Song
of the
Mountains

My Pilgrimage to *Maa Ganga*

Dear Dawn,
Love, Blessings,
Peace

Shakuntala Rajagopal

HUGO HOUSE PUBLISHERS

Song of the Mountains: My Pilgrimage to *Maa Ganga*

ISBN: 978-1-936449-82-8

Library of Congress Control Number: 2015936240

Cover Design and Interior Layout: Ronda Taylor, www.taylorbydesign.com

Cover Painting by: Shakuntala Rajagopal

Hugo House Publishers, Ltd.
Denver, Colorado
Austin, Texas
www.HugoHousePublishers.com

Praise for
Song of the Mountains

"*Song of the Mountains* takes us on an unforgettable pilgrimage through the majestic Himalayas … I have never felt so close to heaven in my life. Entwined within this beautiful travelogue is Shakuntala Rajagopal's own love story, an enduring monument to the only man in her life. At once moving and inspiring, it is a brilliantly written book, a must read for everybody."

— M.P. Ravindra Nathan, M.D.
Editor in Chief, AAPI Journal
Author, *Stories from my Heart*

"Shaku Rajagopal's memoir, *Song of the Mountains*, is a heartfelt and truly human tale of love, loss, and ultimately, rebirth. Told in simple yet elegantly poignant prose, it explores the profound ways in which the people we love define us, and how, in their absence, we must redefine ourselves. This is the most spiritual story I have ever read; it resounded in my heart long after the last page."

— Amy Gail Hansen,
author of *The Butterfly Sister*

Dedication

To Raj, my beloved

Contents

Acknowledgements

I am deeply grateful to my daughters Devi, Molly, and Nimmi, my sons-in-law Don, Suresh, Rasheed, and my grandsons Niko and Travis for their unwavering support of my pilgrimage to *Maa Ganga*, (Mother Ganges), despite their concerns about me undertaking this arduous trip to India, as well as the work it took to produce this book.

All through my trip, my dear husband, Raj, was beside me in spirit, reminding me of our life together, and our everlasting love. Thank you dear one. I miss you a lot.

A million thanks to all my family and friends for encouraging me on my trip as well as in writing this book, and especially Uma Raja who had made the same pilgrimage a few years ago, and who not only mentored me but also cheered me on in writing each section of this very personal story. I am indebted to my cousin Usha for allowing me to use some of her photographs to tell my story.

The confidence Mary Klest expressed in my writing, even with my initial draft, boosted my morale and gave me the push to document my story. The sincere critique that my colleagues at the Barrington Writers Workshop provided helped me immensely with the craft. The workshops at Off Campus Writers Workshop, along with a wonderful quiet time at my Ragdale Foundation retreat in Lake Forest, Illinois, kept me focused to complete this work. Thank you all for the help.

The staff at *Panera Bread* in Algonquin needs special thanks for their kindness during all the hours I sat there immersed in a different world.

I am forever indebted to my dear friend Helen Gallagher for believing in me and her patience in my struggle to balance my travelogue with my spiritual journey.

My gratitude to Dr. Patricia Ross, publisher and editor at Hugo House Publishers is deep and will be felt forever. In editing my work, she understood what was in my head and complemented my expressions with her added words to bring out the best in me. Thank you.

My Love Story

On January 21, 1963 I, Shaku, got married to Raj, my beloved.

Half a century of love is contained in a few drops of my tears as I pen this.

In 1958, the day his father prohibited him from seeing me, Raj declared his love for me. I was seventeen; Raj, nineteen. We pledged our love to each other on a balcony near the Anatomy lab in our Medical College where we were both medical students at the time.

Five years later we got married at the Devi temple by the Shankumugham beach in Trivandrum, my home town in India.

The sun shone bright, the sound of the waves pounding the shore was loud, and the people gathered were even louder. My grandmother, my parents, aunts, uncles, sisters and brother were present. Raj's mom, all nine of his siblings, two brothers-in-law, and cousins were gathered at the front courtyard of the temple. Under a portico roofed with tiles, and surrounded by jasmine garlands, we were wed. His father was not there because he had passed away three years prior, before he witnessed his firstborn son, Raj, become a doctor. That had been a father's dream which had not materialized before he expired.

In the absence of his father, Raj's oldest uncle led him to the gazebo of garlands, and he was seated on a wooden plank with a white cotton cloth covering it.

My father led me by hand to be seated to the left of Raj. When all were gathered around, I stood up and placed a garland of flowers on his neck as a symbol of choosing him for my husband. He reciprocated and placed a similar garland on mine. Next, Raj tied a gold leaf pendant called *Thali*, strung on a yellow thread, around my neck. It had already been blessed in front of the goddess Parvathi, the main deity at this temple. We exchanged gold signet rings; his carrying my name engraved on it and mine carrying his name. He smiled, since he and I knew we did not need these symbols to lock our lives together forever.

Raj and I celebrated our first wedding anniversary apart. He had to leave me in Trivandrum and travel to Chicago to start his post-graduate residency training in the States. I could not accompany him since I had to complete my required one-year internship in Trivandrum prior to graduating from Medical school. The separation broke our hearts. We wrote regularly. Each letter, (all of them saved and cherished) took up to ten days to reach across the oceans and continents. Seven months later, on January thirtieth, 1964, I was reunited with him.

Since then, every anniversary, practically every day, other than a week of professional meetings, we spent together. Despite our full work schedule we worked hard to never be separated for any length of time. In the absence of any of our relatives in this country, we depended on each other for all our needs. We shopped and cooked and cleaned together. In the beginning, Raj called me at work around lunchtime every day of the week, knowing how homesick I was.

Two months after I arrived, I became pregnant with our first child. We bonded over dreams of a new baby, and prayed together for a smooth pregnancy. We took all our vacations together, except when one of us had to visit a relative who had fallen ill. On the rare occasion we had to be apart, we stayed close in our thoughts and prayers.

Until November 2, 2010. That night twenty two of us, immediate family, and a few close friends huddled close, surrounding our beloved husband, father, grandfather, uncle, and friend with our unadulterated love. With eyes closed, and only a breathing apparatus to provide oxygen, he slowly, without any visible struggle, passed away from us.

The most and immediate traumatic feeling is seeing my face in the mirror without my *kumkum thilakom* on my forehead, *pottu*, as we call the red dot we wear. I had worn the dot continually since I was a girl, as a sign of a Hindu girl and later a sign of a Hindu wife. I won't be wearing it now since Raj is not with me anymore.

I am in transition. I have a hard time changing from Raj's wife to Raj's widow. What does this mean? I know I am the same person. But why does it feel that I am not whole?

Could it be that in giving so much of myself to tend to Raj, especially in the past year, I have forgotten a part of myself? I know I kept myself physically fit and held my head high in order to mentally manage the stress of Raj's medical issues, including his Parkinson's and his cardiac problems. I no longer have to worry about him witnessing my weaknesses. I suppose now I could break down and cry. Where are the tears?

Arriving home from the hospital without my Raj, I was not alone. Our daughters, their husbands or fiancé, our nephew and niece, all stayed at our home that night. They were more than familiar with where everything was located at our house, after our years of hosting family events. Yet, it was good for me to be busy, making sure each had a blanket and a place to sleep.

All the times we had friends or family stay overnight, it was Raj who had walked through the bedrooms to ensure there were fresh towels and took the nightlights out of the cabinets and plugged them in. Just as he needed a light when he woke up at night, he knew our guests would need them too.

But my friends and family could not crawl in bed with me. When everyone was settled, I turned in for the night. It was then that I realized I was utterly alone in the special world where, just days before,

Raj and I had belonged together. Our bed was our special, private oasis where we were safe, knowing we were there for each other. Especially in the past four years we were together in that world exclusively day and night, awake and in sleep. We had shared our lives completely. How was I to fill the presence of one that was literally my other half for all those forty-six years?

I climbed in on his side of the bed. I needed the warmth of his presence, although he had not laid there in the last ten days when he was in the hospital. I knew he would never lie there again. I felt empty but I was also determined to do all he would want me to do. I knew I had to go to bed at least to rest my back and limbs in order to be functional the next day. After nine nights of sleeping on the ICU couch, my body craved the feel of a real bed almost as much as I craved his arms around me. His side of the bed gave me warmth and comfort, even in his absence. It really did not make sense, but then nothing did that night.

And he did speak to me. *"You have to get lotto tickets. We forgot them yesterday."* It *was* Raj talking to me. I heard his voice, as soft as it had been in the past year, but distinct, so there was no confusion in my mind. I sat up straight. The clock said 6:15. I had slept, some. There was no chance of sleeping any more, but it was good that the family was in the house. It forced me to stay in bed at least for another hour.

Tuesday morning. It was my first morning without my Raj in this world. He was still with me, but not where I could see him.

The child's monitor I had used for the past six or seven months blinked in the corner. I would not need it any more. He was not going to fall on his way to the bathroom at 2:00 a.m. Many a night, when I could not sleep, I had carried the monitor with me to my study in the loft. More than once I had run down to his side because he called for me in his sleep, when bad dreams disturbed him. When I heard him call, "Shaku, Shaku," in a hoarse, soft voice, I knew he was having a nightmare. I would gently shake him awake and hold him to my bosom until the fear subsided in his voice. If he was thirsty, he would take a sip of water and go back to sleep. On such occasions, I stayed by his side for the rest of the night.

The next day, still reeling with grief, I was not allowed to drive. So after breakfast, the family gathered to discuss what we had to do to honor Raj. I knew family and friends needed to say goodbye. I knew I had to tell the funeral director about our need to cremate Raj's body, as per our Hindu custom.

My daughters helped me choose clothes in which he would be laid for viewing. We also chose shoes and socks, although we were not certain if they were necessary. Raj was the dapper dresser. His favorites were his monogrammed shirts and fancy ties that he always wore in his younger days. After he retired, he still wore ironed pants and tee-shirts and vests even to go walking at the mall. We made sure we picked a suit he liked and an attractive tie.

Devi, Molly and Nimmi, my daughters, drove me
to the funeral home. I did not know they needed so
many signatures from me. As I signed them all, I
realized that I was now the sole owner of Raj's body.
I had to give permission to procure a death certificate.
My friend had already advised me to request twenty
five "original" copies of the death certificate from the
county. So I did. More signatures were necessary: one
signature to let them embalm the body in preparation
for the wake, one for cremation, and yet another one
for procuring the cremation certificate. When all the
signing details were completed, we were asked to set
the dates for the wake. I said, "Only one day." I could
not bear to be sharing any more time than needed
with the rest of the world. We decided on Saturday,
November 6, 2010, from 2:00 p.m. to 7:00 p.m.

All the while the issue of the lotto tickets was
lingering in the back of my mind. Since my children
were not letting me drive, out of respect for my state
of mind, I had Molly take me to the local tobacco shop
where Raj usually bought the tickets. All of his usual
items: Illinois lotto, Mega and Powerball, "pick-four."
For the last one we had a special string of numbers
that Niko, our nineteen year old grandson used to go
around singing when he was a four year old. Standing
at the counter, I remembered the wide smile on Raj's
face as he waved the one hundred dollars at me that
Niko's numbers had won for him eight months prior.

The Saturday after he died, our family and friends
gathered to say goodbye to Raj.

Laid out in his favorite black suit, Raj looked regal, the patriarch that he was. Serene in his eternal sleep, his face showed no worry lines.

The worry lines, however, were on the faces of our friends who had come from India along with us, and we considered extended family. Our old friends from our medical school in the late 1950s, and the new friends we made in this country from 1970s onwards. They knew how close Raj and I were and all wondered how I would survive Raj's absence. Our family members also worried about me. They needn't have. I felt Raj's presence by my side that night and all other nights since.

At the wake, we spoke of his love, his generosity and above all his naughty sense of humor. All of us had at some point borne the brunt of his jokes and his quick retorts. Though the night was a sad one, by no means was it somber. Peals of laughter could be heard at some corners of the room when someone told a story about Raj. Like the times Raj yelled and swore at our dog *Ajit* when he ran away, and again, when he was finally found.

After the official visitation was over, the immediate family did special rituals as per our beliefs. Rice grain soaked in water and drained, blessed with leaves of the holy blue basil plant was prepared for our final goodbyes. Each of us placed a few grains of rice in his lips, as preparation of his life beyond our world. We paid our respects to our beloved Raj and asked for his blessings in this world.

It was difficult leaving his body at the funeral home, knowing that I would not see his face ever again. His had been the face that was my first joyous vision each morning, and the face that made me smile most often in my life.

Early the following Monday, we gathered at the funeral home.

Our daughter Nimmi, accompanied by her uncles and cousins went to the crematorium. She undertook the challenging function to initiate the cremation. I did not go to the cremation. Devi, Molly, and my sister-in-laws kept me company while the cremation was in progress. I had some peace knowing our Hindu rites were followed as much as possible here, so far from our birthplace. It was not easy to accept the fact I would not hold him close to my body, and his arms would never embrace me again. I do know that I was very fortunate in one regard. The love of my family gave me strength to face this final physical separation from my beloved Raj.

Three days later my daughters and son-in-law drove me back to the funeral home to pick up Raj's ashes, which had been separated into two urns I had given to the funeral director.

I placed one urn containing his ashes in an altar I had prepared in my garage. Every evening at the exact time of sunset, we lit an oil lamp and prayed for his soul and for us to be strong to endure our loss. Our grandsons and many members of the extended family joined me on many evenings.

On Sunday, November 14, 2010, as per Hindu custom, our oldest grandson (sine he was the eldest of the male heirs), Niko, did special prayers to facilitate a smooth transition of Raj's soul from this material world to the heavenly abode. The rest of our family joined him in placing flowers around the urn and in saying the prayers.

In Raj's very special twenty-eight year old Mercedes Benz that he truly loved, Niko sat holding the urn containing the ashes of his beloved *Appoo*, the name Niko called his grandfather. I drove them to the closest flowing waters, the Fox River.

Custom dictates that the ashes be placed into flowing waters. The idea was to release the mortal remains into a vast area so that it goes back to the elements of the earth without any limits for eternity.

Our Nephew Kannan, Devi, Nimmi, Molly and Travis joined us on the banks of the river. With utmost love and reverence, first Niko, and then Travis, spread the ashes on the waters and all present floated flowers over the river, saying prayers as our tears mixed in with the waters of the Fox River, in a town outside Chicago.

I pondered many days over what to do with the remaining container of Raj's ashes. I had saved this to take to India as soon as possible and immerse them in flowing water in India. Now I had to decide where. I had choices. The holy River Ganges was one option.

But Raj had no special feeling about the river. Other religiously important areas that I knew of held no significance to either one of us.

The dilemma was for me to find a place where I could part with the last of his remains in a place we had bonded when he was alive, yet religiously proper in the fact that the ashes be returned to nature for eternity and be one with the elements of the earth. In nature, I knew he would be close to me wherever I roamed.

I could as well have chosen the waters at North Avenue beach in Chicago. But I didn't. I wanted someplace in our homeland, India, someplace that had deep personal significance.

In retrospect, it wasn't really hard to decide where to go. Raj's ashes needed to be given back to the universe at Kanyakumari, at the very southern tip of the Indian Peninsula. It is where water from the Atlantic Ocean, Indian Ocean, and Bay of Bengal merge together, and the few places on earth I know where you can stand on the same spot and watch the sun rise from the ocean on the east and see the sun dip into the waters of a different ocean on the west. It was always a special place for both of us.

When in crisis, I think we go back to the most distant time in our past when our mind was least turbulent, when in our past we were most carefree. For me it was when I was living under my grandmother's, my *Ammoomma*'s, roof. As a young girl, when I went to Kanyakumari with my *Ammoomma*, I saw the golden sun rise from blue waters and saw the blazing, fiery hot ball sink in the west. You could almost hear a sizzle when it dipped down, way behind the big waves, way beyond where your eyes could envision the end of the world. Even then I had dreamed of a world beyond what I saw in front of me.

Raj too had gone there as a young boy, with his family and his cousins. I have pictures of him as a young medico, as medical students were called, when he went there on a class picnic, with the ocean in the background. He touts a broad smile, the smile of a carefree young man.

The first time Raj and I went to Kanyakumari together was for our honeymoon. We were married on a Monday in January, 1963. It was only two years and two months after his father's demise, so we had not planned on going away on a honeymoon, leaving his mother, a young widow, with eight young children, the youngest not even three years old. The Wednesday morning after our wedding, Raj decided we should all go to Kanyakumari, to the beach, to celebrate our wedding. Being a last minute decision, we could only get three rooms in *The Kerala House,* the hotel set-up run by the Kerala Government. Packed into three cars, the whole family went, Raj and I, my two sisters and their husbands, Raj's eight younger siblings, a niece and a baby nephew. With only three rooms, the two of us took one room, and the rest of the family shared the other two. For years we heard of how we "stole" a room, leaving the rest in the other two very crowded rooms.

Our next visit happened in 1974 when we went to visit our hometown. We had been living in Chicago for close to ten years. Raj gathered as many of our immediate family members as we could together. We rented a bus to take us to Kanyakumari. The ladies were all decked in our two-piece *mundu* and *neriyathyu* outfits, and Raj lined us up on the beach for a group picture. Our sarees waving and our hair blowing wild in the wind, we looked as happy as ever. My mother is not in the picture because she stayed back to watch over my *ammoooma*. I really believe Raj's need to unite and keep the families together came more from the deep pain he had endured from being estranged from his father in the last years of his father's life.

Raj's mother passed away in 1993. We were fortunate to be back in Trivandrum, and Raj was by her bedside when she took her last breath. Raj and I with a few other family members took her ashes to Kanyakumari, and Raj did the honors, submersing the ashes in the water, while I held him close imparting my love and strength. This is how I knew Kanyakumari meant something important to him, and I knew I needed the love and strength of someone close to me as I spread my husband's ashes in the same water.

I remember the last time we were together at Kanyakumari. We got there in time to see the fiery orange ball of the sun dipping into the waters of the

Atlantic to the west. We stayed overnight to await the sun rise from the Bay of Bengal the next morning. Raj came along only because another couple, close friends, was going with us. Knowing him, I am certain we would have returned home after the sunset, saying, "You have seen it before. It will be the same…this sunrise."

So we stayed. At 6:20 a.m. we looked out the East windows. Grey clouds had rolled in and there was no sun to be seen. We walked up two flights of stairs—he could still walk without help—and waited on an open terrace atop the hotel for a glimpse of a golden sun breaking over the waters. It was 8:30 a.m. before the sun broke through the clouds. Not over rolling waters into a clear blue sky, but lazily peeking out of a bank of grey clouds. It was not the blazing, smiling globe of light we had wished for.

Raj laughed, and said to us, "So the Sun played a bad trick on all of you today." That was classic Raj.

I also knew there was another reason why I needed to make the long trip back to the other end of the world to deliver his ashes to the universe. It had to do with the resurgence of the feelings I had as a young bride when I started my life with Raj—all those years ago. For when I married him, I truly gave my life to him, to be his wife, to care for and honor him as my husband and the patriarch of my family.

When I carried his ashes to the ocean in Kanyakumari in January 2011, I was secure knowing I still had part of him with me. I knew well that parting with his ashes was just a physical act. In my heart and in my soul Raj is present forever.

If I knew this, why did it hurt so much? I was unable to even search for an answer to my own question.

I went to Kanyakumari with a whole *parivar*, strong family and friends. When we reached the ocean I walked alone down the slippery steps. These were the same steps of the familiar *ghat* (steps leading either to the ocean or to the edge of the Ganges), I had walked down with Raj many a time in the past, laughing, teasing, splashing each other and holding hands to balance ourselves.

I stepped into the ocean, leaned down, and touched the first wave which reached me with both hands. I placed a few drops of water on my forehead to get the blessing of the ocean's strength. I held a small plastic bag carrying Raj's ashes securely in my hands and submerged myself completely into the waters, asking with respect and humility for the energy of the mighty ocean that lay in front of me as far as I could see to empower me.

I opened the bag with care, and summing up all the love I had shared with him over our years together, I tenderly placed the ashes into the water, chanting prayers and wishing him peace. Then, only then, after I had fulfilled my last duty to his mortal self did I break down and cry.

I came out of the waters feeling half the being, half the energy that I was.

Raj and I had lived as one being, one spirit for so long. Since we were in our teens we had fed off each other's energy. When he stood up for me against his father's opposition to our getting married, I gave him the strength he needed. When his father died Raj was only twenty-one years old. We both had to grow up in a hurry.

When he decided to come to the U.S. for post-graduate training and later decided to stay, I had to be strong to leave my beloved family and follow him. While it was my love for him that made me do it, it was pragmatism handed down from my *ammoomma* that gave me the courage to do so.

In order to find the will and determination I needed to raise a family in a strange land, while holding a full-time job and building a career in Pathology, I had to tap deep into my inner strength. Later in life, when Raj contracted Hepatitis C, had chronic liver disease, and underwent a liver transplant, there were more demands on me mentally and physically. I drew on my deep religious beliefs to sustain my spiritual and physical strength because Raj and the rest of the family depended on me.

I had done my job. Raj was fully one with God. But something was terribly wrong. I felt as I let his ashes go that my energy had seeped into the ocean waters along with his remains.

Suddenly I found myself floating, without an anchor. I returned home to Chicago and performed all my social duties, as expected of me. I listened to family and friends while they expressed their condolence, heard all the stories of Raj from them and told some of mine. I looked up to the skies and said. "Do you hear what we say about you? Are you laughing at us up there?"

When I was alone at last, at night, the tears flowed. The stream of paperwork continued: trusts, wills, taxes. The inevitables. I handled all that. But what about the issues in my head? Who was to handle them? I had all this time on my hands, but, again, I felt the ocean had drawn my energy away.

In my daily meditation time, my question was how to become a productive member of society again. I had options of volunteering at the retirement home in my area. I knew in my heart that being someone else's caretaker after all those years with Raj was not the answer. Although my head did not admit to it, I was past seventy years in age, and while I was quite healthy and able, I did not feel energetic at the moment.

I realized I had to go deep into my past, *before* Raj and me, to the time as a young girl learning about life from my parents and my *ammoomma*—and not just think about it but really go back to where I had been carefree and strong. Yes, that was it, go deep into my past and draw upon the youthful resources to go forward in my life, alone. But how do I do that successfully?

CHAPTER 1

My Pilgrimage to
Maa Ganga

September, 2011

I was at a crossroads in my life.

It had been a year since my dear husband, Raj, passed away. For his wake, I helped prepare Raj's memorial card, and I quoted words I knew in *The Bhagavad Geetha*, the book of advice from Lord Krishna, considered the Bible for the Hindus.

For the Soul, there is neither birth nor death.
He is not born, nor does He die;
After having been, He again ceases not to be.
Unborn, Eternal, Changeless and Ancient,
He does not perish when the body perishes.

In the many years I had studied my religion, and long hours of pondering the philosophy and the message of Hinduism, those words had made an impact in my mind and in my thoughts.

But in the time of loss and crisis it was a steep challenge to convince my heart of what I had thought I was sure of until then.

Even though I tried to fall back on my religious strength to cope with the loss, nothing worked. I was inconsolable. I knew I had to go deep into my past in order to move forward.

New beginnings need empowerment from within, and I decided to seek help from above to attain such empowerment. After my dear Raj passed, I felt my life was shattered, and I was searching my heart, mind, head, and soul for a way to rebuild, and find meaning in my life. I needed a way to help find a path for me to move forward. I needed something that would provide me a sense of rebirth. I knew where I needed to go. The question was, could I do it without my beloved and at the ripe age of seventy?

As I was flying to South India nine months earlier, when I took Raj's ashes to the ocean at Kanyakumari, I was confined in an airplane at thirty five thousand feet. I had fourteen hours to ponder what I could possibly do to go on without Raj. It dawned on me that I had wanted to immerse myself in the waters of The Holy Ganges River, *Maa Ganga*, or Mother Ganga as we call her, ever since I was a young girl.

In 1951, when I was eleven years old, I took a trip with my *Ammoomma*, my grandmother, to Benares, where *Maa Ganga* bathed the plains of India.

The devout Hindu girl that I was, and a little fanatic, I looked forward to stepping into the holy waters of the River Ganges and procuring her blessings. Hindus believe that when you immerse yourself in the holy waters of *Maa Ganga*, you wash away all sins of the present and past incarnations and your soul will attain *moksha* when you die. Once a mortal soul attains moksha, there is no rebirth, and you are one with God. Thus you escape the repeated mortal rebirth and human suffering. When we reached the *ghat*, a passage or flight of steps leading to the water, I was excited and overwhelmed by the vast body of flowing water and immediately sensed the force of the flowing waters. My heart beat fast as I ran down the steps towards the river.

"Stop right there," my *Ammoomma* called after me. "You are not stepping into that dirty water. If you do, I will break your legs." I burst out crying. I had dreamt of my visit into the waters of Holy River Ganges all through my trip, many miles from my hometown in South India.

My wise *Ammoomma* saw how polluted the river was and forbade me from entering the waters. The water was not clean, not only because of industrial pollution but also due to the Hindu ritual of immersing burning corpses of cremation into the holy river so souls could attain salvation. (Since then the practice has been curbed, and the river has been cleaned up; so I am told.) I returned from that trip without the blessings from the holy waters of *Maa Ganga*.

Maa Ganga, Mother Ganges, had been calling me back ever since then. My true wish was to go to Gangotri, where the River Ganges originates, where the melting snows come down from the glaciers in the Himalayas, where the water is pure and unadulterated by humans, and the air is known to be the purest in the world.

I had the feeling that by getting my blessings from *Maa Ganga* at her unsoiled sparkling origins, I would also honor *my ammoomma's* wish of "not stepping into the dirty waters." At the height of over ten thousand feet above sea level, and being heavily snow-covered from November to April each year, the place is not accessible for occupancy, industry or any source of pollution. In addition, the mudslides make it even harder to access, thus leaving the area clean and safe from the danger of contamination by humans.

Many a time in the eighties and nineties, I suggested a trip to Gangotri. Raj was not interested. He said. "Are you crazy? Why would you want to go up that high and end up with breathing problems? You can go without me. I will stay safe at sea level." So we never went. I could have gone without Raj, but, I wouldn't, mainly because I wanted him to get the blessings along with me, and also because I felt selfish about leaving him alone for such a personal goal.

But, he was no longer with me. This would be one of my first major decisions in life I have made without him. The waters of the Ocean, at Kanyakumari had not only drained my energy, it had also imparted the turbulence into my whole being. The more I thought about it, the stronger I felt that by immersing myself in *Maa Ganga*, it would be a fitting baptism into my new life without Raj.

A new life without him had to begin from the deepest part in my soul to be worthwhile. It all made sense. What better place to go than on a pilgrimage to get *Maa Ganga*'s blessings than at her core of origin from the *Gomukh Glacier*, where she originated in the Himalayan ranges, in the northern-most part of India? As she flows from the melting glacier to Gangotri, there is a temple for the Goddess Ganga. I decided it didn't matter how old I was. I had to go to bathe in *Maa Ganga*'s healing waters.

September 20, 2011
Maa Ganga in the Himalayas

*A **Pilgrimage** is defined as a Journey to a shrine or other sacred place undertaken to gain divine aid, or as an act of thanksgiving or penance.*

There is a pilgrimage that thousands of Hindus take every year that includes the holy headwaters of the Ganges. It's called the sacred Char Dham. It includes four important temples sites, Yamunotri, Gangotri (where the headwaters lay), Kedarnath and Badrinath and it is a dream for every religious Hindu to complete this pilgrimage.

The Char Dham is located in the Indian state called Uttarakhand, the "Land of Celestial Beauty." It is fabled to be endowed with the awesome natural beauty and calm serenity of the majestic Himalayas. The state is studded with stunning snow covered peaks, glorious glaciers, alpine meadows, crystal clear lakes, holy rivers and exotic flora and fauna.

Δ **Trivandrum:** My hometown, where I lived until I was 23 years old.

* **Delhi:** My Pilgrimage to *Maa Ganga* in Uttarkhand in 2011 started from Delhi.

* The map has been sourced from MapsofIndia.com with due permission.

These four most sacred pilgrim centers of India nestle amidst the lofty peaks of Garhwal Himalayas. The four ancient temples mark the spiritual sources of the four sacred rivers: The Yamuna, (at Yamunotri), The Bhagirathi Ganga, (at Gangotri), The Mandakini (at Kedarnath), and the Alaknanda (at Badrinath).

I was well familiar with the *Char Dham*, and while I believed in the sacred journey, I was fully convinced my pilgrimage was going to be specifically to go to the source of *Maa Ganga*'s holy waters in the Himalayan Mountains.

I knew well that this journey would require everything I had in me, my physical strength, and my strong faith I had in the Goddess Ganga. It was an extremely arduous trip through very dangerous parts of the high Himalayas, and I would face very cold temperatures along the way.

When you are in Uttarakhand on this pilgrimage, it is easy to believe that Lord Brahma, while creating the world, reserved the best place for his fellow deities. Uttarakhand is also called the Dev Bhoomi, or abode of the Gods, as it is the land of great pilgrimages. It is fitting that such a spot should become the home of generations of enlightened and sincere seekers after Truth. To the former it provides a life of bliss in oneness with God; to the latter, it affords opportunities for the study and practice of Truth.

The Char Dham pilgrimage is even more meaningful for me, coming from Kerala, the southernmost state of India, because it was Adi Shankara, one of the most revered sages of India who not only revived these four temples, but also unified the philosophy and thoughts for this route of temples between North and South India. He came from the Kerala State, as I did, and he travelled the temple route three times in the 8th Century, A.D.

The completion of this trip in the order that the temples are mentioned is not possible by all who undertake this because the perilous route over mountain roads combined with the flash floods caused by snow melts and the unpredictable mudslides make many a group return to the base camp without completing the four Char Dham visits.

Once I decided I was going on this sacred pilgrimage, I knew I would need help. I enlisted my three maternal cousins from Trivandrum, Usha, Valsala and Bindu to accompany me on the trip. Bindu's husband Sashibhooshan and their son Kannan also agreed to join us. My sister-in-law Susheela heard about our journey and wished to come with us. I agreed it was more meaningful to go with family on this special journey.

The plan was that we meet in Delhi; from there we would start the journey to the Himalayas on the night of September 23, 2011. The trip would take us to the four main temples, travelling by bus five to ten hours a day to reach each of them. We were also told that once our bus reaches the temple vicinity, we had to trek five to seven miles up to reach mountain peaks between 10,000 and 12,500 feet to get to the temple in each area. We would return to Delhi on the eleventh day.

Realizing I would be celebrating my seventy-first birthday during this sojourn, I had to convince my daughters and sons-in-law that I would be all right and promised that I would ask my cousins in the group if I needed help. They had no doubt that I could make it physically. As Nimmi, my youngest, put it, "We have to be afraid and worry about you, because you are not afraid." Devi, the older daughter reminded me that since I had not needed any hospitalization since I was forty-two, and that was for a scheduled surgical procedure, she wished to keep me safe, and not see me in a hospital bed for a long time to come. Molly, my third daughter, whom I thought would be the least worried, was tied up in knots just imagining the rigors of the trip.

Once I convinced them why I had to take this pilgrimage they let me go. They knew I was unhappy, and the fact that my cousin Usha was a doctor, and they knew her very well, certainly helped my case.

September 20, 2011
From Chicago to Delhi

I checked in with American Airlines at Chicago's O'Hare airport for the first leg of my journey to the Himalayas. As I waited for the boarding call, Nimmi snapped a picture with her phone of my long nails painted in red, and sent it to her sister and cousins. She got a big kick of how, even for a pilgrimage, I was well-groomed and color coordinated. She made me laugh.

But on the airplane, I was in tears, remembering how just a year and a half ago, Raj and I had made a similar trip to Trivandrum, South India, to visit family and friends. This was only the second time I was travelling to India without Raj in the last twenty three years.

Once in the air, I could not lift myself above the sad cloud that had descended on me.

When I arrived in Delhi, a great treat awaited me in a tiny form. My grand-niece had delivered a baby girl just five days prior, and the sign of hope this tiny girl presented was a good omen for my journey to the Himalayas as well as my journey forward without Raj in my life.

When my niece placed her granddaughter in my hands, the beautiful little face and the bright dark eyes surveying me, even at that young age, lightened my mood. I wondered, what was she thinking when she saw a new face? Do her eyes know my pain? I worried that I would shroud her in sadness, but then told myself by the time she was old enough to know of loss, she would have forgotten our first encounter. That relieved my anxiety. For now, we were together, four generations of women from seventy years to six days old. Hope for the future, certainly.

The last time I was in Delhi was in 2008, and Raj was with me. Our sole purpose was to visit our niece Laila and family. No sightseeing, we had done that many times; also no shopping, Raj did not feel up to it and I had done mine in Trivandrum, resulting in a very relaxed stay with family.

This time when I arrived in Delhi without my husband, my despair was quite evident. Spending time with our niece and family, the cloud of grief hanging over me showed a glimmer of hope shed around it by the new life and the gurgling sounds of the baby.

As I shared a meal with Laila, we talked of how Raj always resisted tasting anything new. On our visit in 2008, when Laila served yogurt with barotas, unleavened wheat bread cooked over a griddle, Raj frowned, because he was used to eating barotas with chicken curry. Once Laila coaxed him to try it, he smiled, because he really enjoyed the taste. When we returned to the States, however, Raj still wanted chicken curry with his barotas.

We all laughed when I told them that story. Suddenly, without warning I had a tight feeling in my chest, and I had trouble breathing. I made excuses to escape from the room and closed myself in the bathroom for a while. When the grip on my chest let go, and I could breathe normally, I returned to the table. I was able to converse with them without giving away my misery without Raj.

I wondered if I would ever feel completely comfortable anytime soon, to be travelling anywhere or visiting anyone without Raj.

I still enjoyed the warm comfort of my family. They were safe; the journey I was about to undertake had many known pitfalls—one of which was simply travelling by bus on steep mountain roads. Buses were known to fall into the steep ravines. Landslides could happen unexpectedly. It was tempting to stay in the comforts of what was safe, yet, I knew I had to breakout and go on to start my quest in the Himalayas. That was my mission, and I had to fulfill it.

September 23, 2011
Delhi to Rishikesh to meet *Maa Ganga*

Our small party of seven met the rest of the pilgrims we would travel with at the travel agency offices in Delhi on a Friday evening. We were warned that one leg of the trip might not happen because there were landslides between Gangotri and Kedarnath. Hopefully, the roads would be repaired by the time we arrived at that leg of the trip.

Our co-travelers were mostly younger than I: a few couples, some single men, two groups of four and six men, and a family of six, including older grandparents, young parents and two boys, whom I later found out were nine and ten years old. The owners of Panicker's Travels, whose tour buses and guides were taking us on this trip, were related to Sashi, my cousin's husband. They personally welcomed me for the trip and presented me with a bag of apples for the road. I was touched. It certainly was a good omen of a safe trip to look forward to.

Our first stop was at a Ganesha temple in Delhi itself, not far from where we started. Lord Ganesha is the elephant-headed deity who gets rid of any obstacles. We presented him with offerings of prayers, flowers and special food items, the customary ritual any Hindu does before any major undertaking. I would not have proceeded with asking for Lord Ganesha's blessing. This was expected to be a difficult one and we needed all the blessings we could get.

After we offered our prayers at the Ganesha temple, a priest blessed both our buses with an aarti, a ritual of pooja where a tray of flowers with the flame of a lit camphor cube is waved in circles in front of the buses. The strong scents of camphor lit for the aarti, and the chanting of prayers by the priest put me in a peaceful, quiet mood for start of the trip.

I was remembering the time when my father and mother took me on a trip to visit a few special temples in Kerala, South India, before I left to come to the United States. For a whole week we went, offering prayers and obtaining blessings from various Hindu Deities at the temples to ensure a bright future for me, their first-born child, who was leaving the nest to join my husband, who had already arrived in America seven months earlier.

I was grateful I felt calm for the start of this new pilgrimage because the bus ride that followed through the outskirts of Delhi was bumpy, and the constant blowing of horns by the delivery trucks on the road was noisy. Sleep was out of question.

Later I was glad I had not fallen asleep. If I had, I would have missed what I saw that night. At 2:00 a.m., I got the first glimpse of the mountain ranges, silhouetted against a dark blue sky, with tinges of a lighter blue at the very top. From the window of the moving bus, the distant peaks were dark and ragged. A bright sliver of a waning moon showed up in between, playing hide-and-seek between the trees and the darkness of the night.

The ragged peaks foreshadowed things I had not experienced before in my life. While it was exciting and I was not one to be afraid of any new experiences, I felt an apprehension in the air. Maybe because my nerves were more sensitive due to my acute sadness, or maybe because I was not used to going places without my Raj, but I kept thinking, would we even complete our trip without interruption from forces of Mother Nature? I prayed to the Gods to keep me and my fellow pilgrims safe and to help us complete the intended trip.

Forty seven years ago when I left my home in South India to join Raj in Chicago, I was twenty three years old and the trip across half the globe, while it should have been scary, was not. I was too excited and I knew Raj was there waiting for me. I was not scared.

I had no husband waiting for me at the end of this trip. The ragged peaks I saw were awe-inspiring but also foreboding. I not only was apprehensive about reaching Gangotri and being able to get Ganga's blessing but also about making it back safely to see my grandchildren again.

September 24, 2011
Rishikesh

At 3:30 am, we reached our first stop, Rishikesh. We had rooms in a three-story hotel. With no elevators, we had a hard time getting our bags up the stairs to our rooms, although the young men in the group, two cooks and two helpers with them, assisted us. My cousin Usha and I shared a room. Two cots with light beds on them and somewhat threadbare, but clean white sheets, and two very thin pillows were all that were in the room. An attached bathroom had running water but no water heater. We were told hot water would be brought later for our morning baths.

From the balcony of my room, I saw the peaks of the Himalayan ranges silhouetted against a clear night sky under a silvery-bright quarter-moon. I recognized a brilliant star beside the moon as Jupiter, the planet my favorite astronomy website had stated would dominate the night sky in the latter part of 2011 and into the early months of 2012. I had read that Jupiter's gift is to guide you to your highest fulfillment and happiness. As the planet of expansion, some of its pathways are through learning, travel, challenges and philosophy. As I was falling asleep I wondered what it meant to me that Jupiter was ruling the sky that night.

I had barely slept for three hours when one of our cooks loudly announced from the end of the corridor that morning coffee was ready. It was a perfect beginning for the first day of a long-awaited trip, being treated to a cup of hot, already sweetened coffee. The sunlight was barely peeking through against a foggy morning sky. I quickly freshened up, and along with my family members, walked across the yard of the Dayananda Swami Ashram toward a temple on the banks of the River Ganga.

Here, at Rishikesh, the River Ganges flows in full force. The melting glaciers from four different origins of the Ganges merge at different Prayags, or Unions, and the sacred river leaves the Shivalik Mountains in the Himalayas to descend to the plains of northern India as The River Ganges.

The rumbling sounds of the waters reached my ears two blocks before I even saw the river. *Maa Ganga* came into my sight as a vast body of fast-flowing water, totally grey under a dense fog. The fog rolled like clouds over the rising and falling waves as she cascaded over large rocks, forming white foam and eddies. It was an eerie sight I saw, as I stood at the top of a bank of wide stone steps that led down towards the river and the bathing ghat. The waves in the river were forceful and loud as any waves in the ocean. It caused more turbulence within me, and I was not sure I would find any peace by the shores of the raging waters of Ganges in this region.

The opposite bank of the Ganges seemed invisible, unclear because of the heavy, hazy fog, and a lazy sun was barely visible over a misty morning mountain top, which seemed far away.

My heart skipped a beat. I thought of the very first time I had seen *Maa Ganga*, sixty years ago. It was way down in the plains at Benares, and memories of my dear *Ammoomma* who took me there, rendered my eyes moist. That was the time I was not allowed to step into the waters of the holy Ganga.

Finally, the time had come when I could seek *Maa Ganga's* blessing in person, at Rishikesh. This time I walked carefully down the twenty-plus steps to the water. Covered by the fog, the river appeared grey-blue, and the rushing, rumbling waters set my heart racing and my head reeling with the excitement.

Heeding to the caution of my cousins, I gently stepped into the water and gathered the Ganga jalam, Ganges water, in my cupped hands. With utter reverence to *Maa Ganga*, I poured it over my head and touched my eyes with it. My eyes were already wet from tears of joy. Now my face brimmed with a smile of satisfaction. I had been touched and blessed by *Maa Ganga*.

Even as I stepped into the cold water, my heart warmed up and my body tingled at the realization of reaching *Maa Ganga* after waiting for sixty years. As I closed my eyes and thanked God and the Universe for making this happen, I felt a stab of pain, knowing that Raj was not beside me to see my face. He would have said, "Oh! Now you can rest assured you will get Moksha, salvation, and go straight to heaven when you die."

I stood by the river banks for a while, watching two ladies offering flowers and lighting lamps in honor of Ganga Devi, Goddess Ganga. Since we were with many other pilgrims, I could not proceed to take a bath in the river at this site. I had to be satisfied with the hope of immersing myself in the river, at a later time during our trip.

A temple dedicated to Lord Shiva stood at the top of the steps. The walls were painted white and despite the foggy morning, looked dramatic, touting stripes of red paint along the top borders. Red stripes were seen all along the corners of the building too. In the lower part of the building, all four walls had vertical red stripes up to about two feet high. I entered the temple, and offered prayers at Lord Shiva's sanctum. As is usual in all Hindu temples there was a place dedicated to Lord Ganesha. In addition, in honor of Ganga Devi, a special sanctum was present. I prostrated in front of Devi to bless our pilgrimage. We took part in the morning pooja rituals and this made me feel quite at home. When the temple bells rang loud, I felt their sounds carried my prayers high on to heaven.

Returning to the hotel from the river, the aroma of a simple but savory vegetarian breakfast welcomed us, served outside in the courtyard under a Banyan tree. Idlis, steamed rice cakes, were the main item. We ate them dipped in Sambar. Sambar is a spicy hot mixed-vegetable curry of potatoes, cucumbers, eggplants and cut beans all simmered in a mixture of red peppers, turmeric, asoefetida, tamarind juice, and coriander. While we pilgrims slept, the cooks who came with us had prepared our breakfast. I felt pampered to be thus catered to. As we ate our breakfast, the cooks were already busy preparing our lunch. After breakfast, we set out to visit Rishkesh and the different temples in the area.

As a youngster growing up in South India, I learned of Hindu culture, and the two major Epics taught were The Ramayana, and The Mahabharata. In both legends, the characters either lived or went through the same regions of the Himalayas, at some point in their journeys on earth. Rishikesh and the surrounding areas have many special temples closely linked to both Epics, and the holy river played a very important part in the evolution of the historical sites. I was excited to be visiting the places I had heard about in my childhood, long, long ago.

The sun had come up and chased away the fog, leaving a clear day and blue skies for our enjoyment. The day was spent visiting Shivananda Yoga Ashram. The ashram had a temple for prayers, meditation halls, and dorm-like arrangement of rooms for the resident yogis, as well as visitors who came to learn Yoga and meditation, or for a quiet respite from busy lives. This was one of the ashrams the Beatles had visited while they trained in Transcendental Meditation with Maharishi Mahesh Yogi at his own ashram, just a few miles from where we stood.

After touring the Ashram grounds, we walked over Lakshman Jhula, a 480-feet suspension bridge over the River Ganga, to the opposite banks of the river. There we reached sacred temples dedicated to Lord Sri Rama, Lord Shiva, and Lord Ganesha. This area and these temples are steeped in the history, I had heard told from both Ramayana and Mahabharata. Standing in the Himalayan foothills listening to our guide go over the stories felt fantastic. I closed my eyes and the voices of my aunt and mother recounting them resonated in my head, and goose bumps covered my arms and neck.

At the temples, we made offerings of flowers and camphor which we purchased from the adjacent shops, and in return, we received red kumkum powder and yellow sandalwood paste as blessed offerings. The smell of incense and camphor burning for the aarti and pooja rituals, mixed with the clanging of temple bells created a surreal atmosphere for me. The undertaking of this sacred pilgrimage had begun, and the full significance of that hit me in that moment.

Walking from one temple to the other, cows, goats and dogs roamed freely among us. The cows were decorated with garlands and wore red kumkum powder and yellow sandalwood paste, the same signs of blessings from the temple that we wore on our forehead. The animals did not bother us, and they seemed not to be bothered by our presence.

After a peaceful morning of prayers and lessons in history, we rode a boat across the Ganges to return to our hotel. A new knowledge I acquired was how water sports had developed in the river, including white-water rafting. We did see some rafts speed by. It was a surprise for me.

We found our lunch all prepared and our cooks waiting to serve us. Rice was the main dish. This was served with dhal, a cooked lentil sauce flavored with turmeric, cumin and red pepper, spices which make it tasty, but also help spice up our immunity (turmeric), and our digestion (cumin). Also, red pepper is known to stoke the fire in our gut and help digestion as well as lift our spirits. If too much is used, it will certainly make one cry.

Again, we ate in the courtyard, with colorful birds perched on large Aspen trees. On the roofs around the courtyard, and atop the trees, medium-sized monkeys, some as small as a six-month-old child and some as big as a two-year-old child, sat watching us eat. When someone gave them food, they grabbed it, climbed up the trees and sat happily eating it until another one threatened to steal it. They jumped up and down on the branches, shaking the whole tree, and swung from one branch to the next, just ten feet above us. The people who lived there assured us they were harmless, despite the ruckus they made.

Around 2:00 we were packed, the buses loaded, and we were on our way to Barkot, the next town where we would stay that night. Every trip started with our guide, Mr. Chouhan, invoking Lord Ganesha. We repeated after him, "Lord Ganesh Ki Jai" (Victory to Lord Ganesha.) This was followed by invocation to Goddess Yamuna, the goddess of the river Yamuna, Goddess Ganga, the goddess of the river Ganges, and to the deities of the temples we were visiting.

A group of eight pilgrims who belonged to a meditation center in South India led us in chanting prayers. Then I had a chance to lead them in a few of my favorite prayers. Although I cannot carry a tune, I knew well that you don't need perfection when rendering your prayers. What you lacked in tune, you made up in fervor. God is all-embracing and all-forgiving.

The route we took wound along the banks of the Ganges. The winding roads were beautiful, and when the sun shone on the trees the brilliant greens were breathtaking. The roads were narrow and steep. When the bus turned at acute hairpin turns and stomach-churning curves, the steep drop-offs were visible up close. When I saw that some of them were over hundred feet deep, an involuntary prayer escaped my lips. After about two hours, we came to a fork in the road and we took a turn to go Northwest on our way to Yamunotri, the first temple of the Char Dham, and the origins of the River Yamuna.

CHAPTER 2

My First Transformation at Yamunotri

September 25, 2011

"Chai, coffee! Chai, coffee!" We were awakened by the welcome sounds of the cook's assistant calling to come and get our morning coffee. My phone showed 4:00 a.m. My cousin Usha and I walked out from our motel room and in the cold pre-dawn darkness saw the young man with a huge coffee pot perched on a wooden stool, from which he filled the steel tumblers with coffee. The steaming hot coffee with the sugar already added gave me the oomph needed to get a head start on the day.

Soon after serving us coffee he came back with buckets of hot water for each of us. We took turns to have quick baths after mixing the cold water from the taps with the hot water in the buckets in order to give us enough bathing water. We hurriedly repacked our belongings and boarded the bus to proceed on to Yamunotri.

On the road to Yamunotri

We started up the mountain on the westward side, and as the bus made a turn, our eyes awoke to the sight of bright yellow sunshine on an opposite mountain, giving the evergreens a golden-green hue. We and our bus still travelled in darkness, because we were on the west side of the mountain. It was at least thirty minutes later that we came into the path of the early morning sunshine.

At first it was difficult to keep track of where we were. The mountains here were of such great heights, and we ourselves were travelling approximately seven thousand to eight thousand feet above sea level, and this skewed the position of the rising sun. I could not figure out if we were facing east or west. Suddenly beams of early morning sunlight filtered through the tall firs silhouetted against the streaming white light, and the whole world burst into the white sunlight. The mountain firs standing guard above us now gleamed pure green, and the golden hue was almost forgotten instantly. I knew once again which direction I was going.

Ascending the mountain made me feel different. The movement upwards seemed to physically help me to get out of the doldrums I had settled into, the low place that I had sunk into since I lost Raj. The lack of our morning routine and the memories of our mornings together were the source of heartache for me each morning. Making morning coffee for Raj, fixing him breakfast, making sure he ate his food and swallowed his many morning meds without choking: all these rituals which kept me busy in the mornings were now missing in my life without Raj.

The upward movement of this trip gave me a symbolic thrust to direct my energies toward what I needed to do with the empty time. I hoped that, like the sun bursting through and guiding our way, maybe this pilgrimage would help me channel new intentions for what I needed to do to get over the hurt that filled my morning hours.

The awakened earth and bright sunlight brought out the rhythms of many prayers from us pilgrims and we took turns leading the group in the chants: "Jaya Ganesha, Jaya Ganesha Jaya Ganesha Paahimam…," We call to Lord Ganesha to be victorious and give us safe haven….

Then we were lead through a prayer to Lord Shiva: "Shivoham, Shivoham, Shri Valsa Yogam…," We are one with you, Oh Lord Shiva, we deserve to enjoy your blessings….

Often our songs were broken up when the wheels of the bus hit ruts and rocks. The act of surrendering to the divine powers through our prayers mitigated any apprehension we felt about the tricky journey on the narrow mountain roads.

Climbing up the mountain, away from the wide flowing river, the shrubs and trees changed. The flowering shrubs that touted clusters of red and purple flowers were replaced by taller trees with wide branches. Under these umbrellas of the green tops, vendors sat trading handmade necklaces and bags with bead-work adorning the surfaces. The crystal beads shone bright green, blue, and yellow and the white and red beads glittered like diamonds and rubies in the clear sunlight. I was reminded that the people that lived in these hills depended on us the pilgrims for their livelihood.

Scattered along the roadside we passed small coffee-shops called dabbas. Usually, one half of the dabba housed a kitchen where they prepared tea by boiling milk in aluminum pots with cardamom pods added for flavor. Vegetable samosas sizzled in hot oil. These are snacks made of boiled smashed potatoes mixed with sweet peas, spices including hot peppers, all rolled into a ball, wrapped inside a soft dough skin, and fried deep and long until the outsides were a light brown color. The smell of the food wafted into the bus and made me hungry.

Two hours into the morning, we stopped at a dabba. The dabba building hung precariously over a wide, open valley. I walked out on to the balcony and the scene that greeted me took my breath away. I waved to my cousins to come join me outside. Five mountain peaks rose high in front of us, and the lower range of mountains closer to us were covered by evergreens, firs, pines and cedars.

The Himalayan cedar is known as deodar, or Devadaru. Deva, the first half of the Sanskrit term, means divine, or deity, and Dāru, the second part, is related to the words durum, druid, tree, and true.

Deodar is a holy tree with known medicinal values, and mentioned in the epic poetry of India, set in three hundred to five hundred A.D. Its wood has a strong aroma. It is used for incense, and its cedar oil is also an excellent insect repellant.

A waterfall and its river beneath us completed the picture, and I was convinced that a divine paintbrush decided to treat our eyes to the majestic scene to carry with me for the rest of my life. Standing still on the balcony of the dabba, I closed my eyes and listened to the song of the River Ganga as she rushed over the rocks way down in the valley, below us. The sound of the water reverberated from the valley up to where we stood, about one hundred feet above the valley floor.

I had read that if you listen closely you could hear the song of the mountains. But that morning, I heard no music in the mountain winds. Maybe they were not carrying the song of the mountains, or maybe I was not primed or ready to receive that special music, yet.

For breakfast at that dabba I had the freshly made samosas and avoided any fresh green salads. I only drank hot tea. Having left India over four decades ago, I did not have the immune powers in my body to survive any inherent health problems that exist in places away from more modern restaurants and pasteurized milk. But the people! The workers chatted easily with us travelers. Their broken English and my broken Hindi made a fine mish-mash.

Hindi is not my primary language. Malayalam is. Once we were free from the British rule, Hindi was made our "National" language. It was mandated that all schools in the new Republic of India teach Hindi. With twenty-eight plus languages with full grammar and their own alphabet, and another thirteen or so dialects, English was the only common language in all the states. So, the Indian government declared English the "Official" language of free India. The beauty of the Indian people lay in the fact that despite the oppression by the British rule, when it mattered most, the free India assimilated the already learned English language, and used it to unite the different kingdoms of India that formed the Republic of India.

We had been following the course of the River Ganga up to now. After breakfast our bus took a westward course to follow the course of the River Yamuna. Because of the way the mountain peaks aligned themselves it was necessary to take a circuitous route and go in the opposite direction before we went eastward to reach Yamunotri.

The clear blue waters of the River Yamuna rushing over dark rocks were totally different from the greenish waters of the River Ganga we had followed earlier. We crossed the river on a bridge which looked as if it could use a major overhaul. Travelling down a winding road on one side of a mountain, we crossed the river again to climb up yet another mountain to make it to the origin of the sacred River Yamuna. The closer we got to the river the roaring waters made even the most talkative person on the bus go quiet.

My mind was quite turbulent all morning with thoughts of Raj. Riding the bus, hearing the roar of the river, seeing the power of the water in the land-slides evident on the mountain slopes, all made me realize that changes and disruption of routine in our lives are similar to changes that are usual and normal happenings in nature. It was small consolation, yet it made me realize that as we were now ascending the mountain, tracing our path upwards from where River Yamuna originated, I too had to first go deep into the origins of my grief to really address it before I could get over it the best I could and gain strength from this pilgrimage to go forward. That was the only way I could find meaning and live a productive life.

We were scheduled to stop over in the town of Barkot, where the road bifurcates before the climbs to Yamunotri on one side, and the second one to Gangotri. By sundown we arrived at our village.

While we unpacked and caught up with stories about the temples at Yamunotri and Gangotri, our cook and his helpers had prepared dinner. Our dinner included fresh-cooked cauliflower, and rotis, flat, unleavened wheat bread that looked similar to tortillas. With a somewhat spicy tomato curry added, the meal was tasty and fulfilling. After dinner, many of us sat in the veranda of the hotel building, exchanging stories of why some of us were taking this journey.

My family group made up seven members out of the twenty pilgrims in our bus. Then there were four couples, also from our home state of Kerala, friends who had made other pilgrimages together. Four of them had done this same pilgrimage in the past. There was a group of three men, from Andhra Pradesh, north and east of our state, and a family of two brothers with their wives and sons and their parents.

All in all the pilgrims ranged from nine and ten year olds to twenties and thirties and sixties and seventies. The young couple was taking their older parents on a special trip to the four temples of the Char Dham Yatra, and the young children were trudging along, not quite understanding the significance of the journey. There was a middle aged couple, the husband had suffered from cancer of the lung, and was in remission. This trip was fulfilling an offering, a promise they had made when praying for a cure for his cancer.

The next morning we went from Barkot to the base of the mountain from where we would climb up closer to the origins of the River Yamuna. The town of Yamunotri is on the banks of the river, and there is a temple dedicated to Yamuna Devi, the goddess of the river.

The route from Barkot to Yamunotri is not an easy one. The ride took us up from about three thousand to ninety-five hundred feet above sea level. The roads are narrow, and previous landslides made parts of it one-lane only. Riding up the mountains, the awesome power of the rushing water was visible in landslides, where tons of mud and rock had fallen, washing away any vegetation in its path. Where parts of the roads were washed out, there was only one car or bus-width, and the traffic had to be regulated. Efforts of cleanup were visible, including the Caterpillar tractors from the U.S. parked alongside some repaired roads. To add to the problems, stubborn herds of bullocks and sheep used and blocked the roads, and the trip became outright dangerous.

The road crews we saw worked very hard and fast to restore two-lane roads. In some places human efforts were winning against Nature. We learned to appreciate the expertise and care of the bus driver as he maneuvered the bus, and also the skill of his assistant who had to guide him through some tough, narrow and steep curves.

The crashing noise of the water grew louder as we got closer to the temple. The air was cold, although the snow was only visible on the mountain peaks and not on the grounds yet. I was told that this would change soon, and the entire place would be snow-covered by the middle of November.

Breakfast was served in a thatched building about thirty feet square, with mud floors made smooth with sand and clay tapped down firmly, and bordered all around with wooden logs to contain the sandy mixture. It had no walls, but long logs supported the roof approximately eight feet apart on all sides. Half-walls two feet tall made of bricks that appeared rough and not kilned, surrounded one half of the room. In this area, milk and water boiled in aluminum pots atop two stoves to make tea for us. A few wooden benches filled the other part of the shed, and we took turns sitting down to eat. Two wooden tables held our breakfast of rotis, flat bread made of wheat, and a potato curry with onions. It was mild as to red pepper content, but had a good flavor to it with the coriander, cardamom and turmeric cooked in. The hot tea helped to take the morning chill off for us.

Cows roamed around us, and of course with them came the dropped cow dung as well as the urine. At least they did not come inside the thatched shed. I was glad my daughter Devi had provided me with enough Quick-wipes.

After breakfast we prepared for the climb up to the temple. We were informed the way up to Yamunotri was three and a half miles long and a steep climb uphill. My options were to trek uphill, ride a pony, or get carried up by four people in a doli, a palanquin of sorts, with a wooden seat mounted on bamboo poles. The weather was turning colder, but with the sun shining on us, and me with my light yet warm North Face jacket and hood, felt comfortable to make the trek up the mountain path. I did not have any breathing problems, and I was feeling quite fit.

I chose to walk. But, within the first mile itself the path posed difficulty; I had to climb over stiles and up a set of uneven steps. The rocky slopes were slippery from the deposits from the ponies ahead of us. By now I was about a half mile up, and although I did not develop breathing problems, I did not feel totally comfortable. My goal was to reach the temple, not to prove my fitness.

I mounted a pony for the rest of the ascension to the temple at Yamunotri. The pony's name was Anjali. The young man who managed her told me with pride he was her owner. His name was Ajay.

To my surprise, as I got close to the temple on that cold morning, I saw hot steam come up from part of the river. When I alighted from my pony and walked towards the temple at Yamunotri, I saw that steam arose from the hot springs in the Yamuna. All of us were happy that we were able to bathe in the hot waters. The women had a sheltered area, while the men bathed in a not-so-private, open part of the hot springs. The water was too hot to completely immerse ourselves. We used plastic mugs to pour the water over us and the flowing water appeared clear and clean to do so. After the cleansing bath in waters hotter than the spa at Lifetime fitness center, water that warmed me if just for a short while, I joined my family members to perform a pooja ceremony or prayer service, for the Goddess Yamuna.

It was a two-fold process. A poojari, priest, gathered us family members in a group, and just outside the Sanctum of Yamuna Devi, we proceeded to worship in her temple. The deity of Goddess Yamuna was made of black granite, and by her side, a deity of Goddess Ganga, made of white marble, was also present. In front of a lit lamp, he led us in Sanskrit prayers to get the blessings of Yamuna Devi.

Just before our offerings, the poojari's assistant had each of us place a small cloth bag containing a fistful of rice grains in each bag into the hot springs close to the temple. At the end of our pooja ritual, we went to retrieve the bags of rice, and found that the hot, boiling water had cooked the rice. We then made special of offering of our cooked rice to Goddess Yamuna. After this was blessed at the temple, we got it back as prasadam, food that is a blessed offering.

Standing at the altar of Devi Yamuna, my palms folded in worship, my mind raced back to the Devi temple at Chenthitta, in Trivandrum, where I had started my life of prayers, seventy years ago. I felt a new energy. Or maybe, it was a resurgence of the same energy I had felt when I walked and prayed at the Chenthitta temple, as a young girl.

In the late 1950s, when Raj's father was against Raj marrying me, and our future together was in jeopardy, I had surrendered all my hopes and dreams at the feet of Chenthitta Devi, the deity at that temple, and left it in her divine hands to make my wishes come true. Now, when I needed help to cope with my separation from my dearest Raj, I again laid my burdens in front of the Goddess at Yamunotri. The amazing transformation of my mind from a seventy-one year old to a ten year old, and the renewed enthusiasm within me for this journey overwhelmed me. My eyes blurred, and I stopped breathing for a minute.

I felt my cousin Usha's arm on mine, and she brought me back to the present, leading me down the stone steps.

"Are you hungry enough to eat lunch?" she asked. "Or, do you want to wait until we descend to a lower level? We can get hot tea at the dabba, the one we had passed on our way up," she continued.

I was not hungry. "I feel satiated from all the excitement," I told her in a hoarse voice. Knowing I was a diabetic, Usha made me eat some butter cookies and drink water. We then walked around the temple and looked up at the tall peaks from where the River Yamuna originated. Way up in the rocks it appeared like a trickle of blue water. But by the time she flowed in the precinct of the temple, it was a roaring waterfall, bouncing over dark rocks, emanating wild waves and throwing frothy white foam into the air. We watched the river in awe for a while, until Mr. Chauhan called our group to, "Please come down and board the bus." We knew we had to get going.

We started our descent. I was restless on my pony on the way down. I felt so energized.

On the way down to Barkot, where we were to stay the night, there was an unusual hush within the bus. Maybe it was the soothing effect of the experience at the temple or maybe it was the thin air at the new heights we were travelling in, whatever it was, my fellow pilgrims and I were affected deeply by the ride down on a road wedged between the deep gorge down to the river on one side and the rising mountains on the other.

In the quietude, my mind wandered to the past year of turbulence following Raj's demise. I don't think I will ever forget feeling like I was tossed into the middle of a thunderstorm, more like a paper-storm, with the unending stream of paperwork and the emotional gales of my children and grandchildren, and my fast breathing, as I tried to decide what was best for me.

It was June, 2011, eight months after Raj had passed on. I was trying to put on a brave face to the world. I had to. Whatever we had done together for, and with the rest of the family, I had to take on double duty, now that Raj was gone.

Raj, I miss you in all the ways that matter. In small ways, when I walk into your office, and you are not sitting at your desk. In larger ways when the children come over and we are talking about basketball playoffs, or about the SUV which Nimmi has purchased. When we peruse the most recent art work by Travis and you are not there to see it. Many a time I have to quietly leave the room when your absence hits me without warning.

And then there are those days when the paperwork and the procedures for changing the name on an account get so confusing, I am overwhelmed. Those are not even the worst days. The name change finally goes through, and I am relieved.... but then the day after one of the monthly payments should have been automatically withdrawn from our checking account, (your name is still on all the checking accounts), I find that the MasterCard has not been paid. So, I call. Unbelievable! When the name of the primary card-holder was changed, the agreement to "auto-pay" was null and void. You would think somebody would have the courtesy to include the information in their letter, which confirmed the name change.

Now that I know, I call the credit card company, and pay the proper amount over the telephone, confirm that my credit score is not affected, and breathe again. But with the breath of relief comes a flood of tears. Why did I let you go? If I knew of all the daily unwanted hassles looming before me to go on living alone, maybe I would have fought harder and prayed harder to keep you with me longer. Not that I really believe that my fighting would have changed the outcome. I know well it was your time to go. I fully believe you have a special place close to Almighty God in his heavenly abode.

Eleven months have gone by, and I had assumed a somewhat regular schedule in my life and felt I could stop and breathe. I decided to take stock of my place in this world and the Universe.

As we travelled in contemplative silence, I knew that for this day, if nothing else, I have left all my mortal necessary chores and travelled up these mountains in the hope that my pilgrimage will give me proper perspective and timely strength to face all new challenges.

It was a testament to my determination that I was on this pilgrimage to *Maa Ganga*. It dawned on me that my road to Gangotri was paved with other benefits as well. It gave my heart hope that since I started from a level of six hundred feet above sea level in Chicago, and made it to Yamunotri at a height of nine thousand feet up in the Himalayas in just six days, I could climb out of my state of despair too, if I put my mind to it.

Leaving Yamunotri, we backtracked part of the way we had already traversed to the fork in the road at Tehri. This is where we had gone westward to get to Yamunotri. The honking of car horns to get pedestrians out of the way, combined with people shouting at cars and buses to make way for vendors carrying vegetables in baskets and rice or wheat grains in sacks on their heads, all made for a raucous junction. The cows walking at their own slow pace, and the bullock carts overloaded with more grains and vegetables for the market, made it even more crowded and confusing. The short time of tranquility in our bus was broken.

I was back to civilization with my own challenges.

CHAPTER 3

The Headwaters of the Sacred River: Gangotri

September 27, 2011—Barkot to Uttarkasi

We now followed the road eastward and to the north to Gangotri and the temple there. Although the evergreens were almost the same as the ones we saw on our way to Yamunotri, now other blooming trees holding bunches of white flowers were strewn among the firs and cedars.

Terraced farming with yellow mustard fields scattered the landscape, the undulating yellow flower heads adding a rare beauty to the mountainside. This was unexpected. I did not know they could farm mustard that high up in the mountains.

The last time I saw mustard fields was way down on the flat plains in central India. It was 1999 when Raj and I, accompanied by our neighbors Ken and Vera, travelled through Rajasthan after visiting the Taj Mahal, in Agra. We were not on a stated pilgrimage then. While the guide narrated the story of the Taj, we stood gazing at the beauty of the marble edifice. Tears streamed down my cheeks, and I felt a reverence to the spirit of love that moved Emperor Shah Jahan to build the eternal monument in memory of Mumtaz Mahal, his wife and the love of his life. My favorite poet Rabindranath Tagore called the Taj Mahal "a teardrop glistening on the cheek of time."

Maybe that trip too was a pilgrimage in its own right. In addition to the Taj Mahal we visited the palaces and forts of the kings, the warriors, and the strong ladies who helped form the history of India. The state of Rajasthan was affected greatly by the invasions it endured through the hundreds of years. The people in this region were deeply influenced by the changes in rulership, and the ensuing mixture of Arabic, Parsi and Aryan cultures shaped their mode of survival, as well as their customs and way of life. The food here was also affected by the Arabic and Parsi culinary habits.

Just remembering how special that trip with Raj was, just four years after he had undergone a liver transplant, gave me the shivers. Knowing we would never see those places together again brought a choking sensation to my throat. I said a prayer for him and looked out the bus window, concentrating on the scenery outside so my thoughts wouldn't take me inward any more. It seemed as if the dull ache in my chest would never end.

We came upon an unusual crop of feathery grass about two-and-a-half feet tall, bearing elongated tufts of showy crimson flowers. Lining vast areas of the terraced plots, the crimson flowers posed a dramatic contrast to the various shades of evergreens on the mountain slopes. Our guide Mr. Chouhan did not know the name of the flowers but told us that the flower heads were dried and used for red food coloring, non-toxic and natural.

When we returned to the hotel that evening I fell ill. My stomach churned and I lost all my lunch. This was followed by repeated visits to the toilet. I took my Imodium, which I carried for such occasions. Thank God my cousin Usha is a physician. She examined me and since I did not have a fever, we decided all we needed was rest and a plain liquid diet with water and warm black tea. I did add sugar to the tea, for taste as well as a few calories. In an hour or so, my symptoms subsided. Usha also had a little stronger medicine to help me, and I fell asleep without much discomfort.

The next day we kept my diet simple with broth of cooked rice and more black tea. Our cook and his assistants made sure I had hot tea with sugar any time I needed it. That many miles away from home, I deeply appreciated their kindness. Usha also found crackers for me in a dabha on our way to Uttarkasi, our next stop.

On the Road to Gangotri

Uttarkashi, or Northern Kashi, has the same religious importance as Kashi, or Benares, the renowned pilgrimage center on the banks of the Ganges in the plains of India. Uttarkashi is set on the banks of the Bhagirathi Ganga, at an elevation of 3,904 ft. We crossed the River on an old bridge, and on the opposite shore we came to a hotel, which was much larger than the facade made us believe. The front of the building had a double door, with two windows to the right on the ground floor and three windows to the left. But once we entered the front hall, we saw steps going up and steps going down, just beyond the entryway. To the left a reception area with a couch and television showing a newscast in Hindi. All three levels had many rooms, which although not large, were clean and comfortable.

We placed our possessions in our rooms and walked out on the second floor terrace. From there we got a full view of the River. It was early afternoon, and the sun shining on the river highlighted the river flowing at full force. The wild eddies and currents combined with the thundering rush of the waters noisily proclaimed the power of the River Ganga as it flowed by.

All afternoon my cousins and I strolled through the narrow streets of this unique town. The streets were lined on both sides by small shops carrying items for us to conduct pooja services at the temples we were about to visit, and also for the Ganga Aarti, a special tribute to the river that was close by. The shopkeepers were laid back, not aggressive vendors who pushed their wares. We picked up candies, nuts and fruit. While we walked the streets, the rumble of the water two blocks away reminded us why we were there. We felt totally welcome and at peace, and not at all like tourists in this special place.

The people of this village spoke Hindi and we spoke Malayalam. After we were liberated from the British in 1947, Hindi was made the National Language, and it was mandatory that children all over India learned Hindi in school. Although we understood some Hindi, (me the least, after so many years away from India,) none of us were really fluent in the language. To admire the simple handicrafts in the little shops on both sides of the narrow streets in this quaint town up in the mountains, we did not need to know Hindi. To show reverence to the religious artifacts we were handling, and to pay in Indian Rupees, we only needed smiles and nods on each other's parts.

We picked up brass plaques with reliefs of Lord Shiva polished so bright that the sun reflecting from them flashed on our eyes, momentarily blinding us. Rudraksh beads from a special tree in the Himalayas, strung in garlands of 108 beads each for chanting daily mantras, were available here. I purchased a few for gifts to my older relatives and one Rudraksh garland for my friend Amit, the shopkeeper in the Algonquin store where Raj and I bought our Lotto tickets.

At dusk, we walked a little over a mile up to a temple dedicated to Lord Shiva. On our way up a hill, we saw a public maidan, a playground and park, where children played cricket in one section. Many people walked the perimeter of the park, and some people just gathered here and there to stop and talk. When we reached the temple, we saw large red letters on the white wall of the temple. The writing was in Hindi, It said "OHM

Namashivaya," meaning Praise to the name of Shiva. It is believed that when we do our pranams, paying respect by prostrating on the ground in front of Lord Shiva, he will make our trip to Gangotri the next day go smoothly without any hindrance. We took our own sweet time to stop and say our prayers to Lord Shiva to keep us safe.

The truth is that many a pilgrim has returned from the mountains without reaching the sanctity of Gangotri because the roads up there are often blocked by mudslides and rushing water from the heights. We were told repairs are usually undertaken with the help of large equipment of the Army Corps of Engineers. Even so, not everyone attempting this trip gets lucky enough to make it. The window of opportunity closes without warning, and the waiting cars and buses are totally helpless and at the mercy of the elements in this part of the world.

After the prayers at the Shiva temple, we descended to the river's edge. We took turns doing a Ganga Aarti, using plates holding flowers and lit camphor, doing a pooja to the waters of the Ganga at this place to honor the river. At that special hour when the day is gone, and the night has not arrived yet, the sound of the waters, the hot red flame from the camphor in the tray, and the surrounding rhythm of the prayers uttered in unison by a dozen devotees of *Maa Ganga*, I was taken to a state of bliss from the fact that I had made it so far. But it was also knowing I am not alone in our home without Raj, waiting for him to appear, even if I know fully he is not coming back.

Many a time in the past year, I had stopped in the middle of a room imagining the door opening, and I walk to the door anticipating Raj to enter. The door does not open, and Raj is not there. That is the time I start to panic. Who am I cooking the chicken for? I finish cooking anyway, and then put the pot away. When dinnertime comes, I pretend Raj is sitting at the table with me. I remember how I coaxed him to eat, and made sure he ate as well as he could. So, I take a page from the past, and eat my food. Moderate portions of meat, vegetables and rice. I have to stay healthy for my sake and my children. I know why I am on this trip.

We sat on the steps of the ghat and chanted prayers to Lord Shiva and to Devi. In that enchanting twilight time, I glanced at the faces of my fellow travelers, enveloped by the fragrance from the smoking camphor, and lit by the glow of the oil lamps surrounding the temple. They reflected a certain calm we had attained in the chanting, despite the hectic days we had endured.

We returned to our hotel where the cooks had supper waiting, warm, spicy and tasty. A simple meal of rice, dhal, yellow split peas, and cauliflower curry was satisfying and was appreciated more than a feast of eight items including a meat dish would have been, because we were all so hungry. More so for me after the deprivation of any spicy stuff for a whole day, the day before.

September 27, 2011
Uttarkashi to Gangotri

The way to Gangotri from Uttarkashi followed the banks of the Bhagirathi Ganga as it flowed regally down from the mountain peaks. The distance of about thirty miles took five hours because we were ascending from an altitude of 3,094 ft. at Uttarkashi, to 10,000 ft. at Gangotri. Even where the mudslides had been cleared, the bus route was narrow, and many a time our bus had to stop while we let another one pass. In some places the edge of the road was barely one-foot from the tires of the bus. The land dropped from sixty to one hundred feet below to our side. As long as I did not peer out of the bus too close to the edge, I was okay. When I dared to look down, it took my breath away to see how close the bus was to the edge, and a prayer on my lips was all that helped me breathe again.

I was struck by the intoxicating beauty of the large firs, mottled with patches of low shrubs carrying tiny blue flowers. An occasional clump of cactus and aloe plants dotted the landscape. On the slopes we saw goats, sheep, and cows grazing. The way our bus route intertwined with the flow of the river was fascinating. Sometimes the river was to our right, and after we crossed a bridge, she was to our left for a while. After two hours, we came to a town called Maneri. Here, a dam across the river formed a vast lake, and we could hear the loud gushing sound of the dam waters being released, first for the hydroelectric projects, and then to the neighboring areas for water supply and irrigation purposes.

Even in the holy mountains life was changing and modernizing very fast.

Mr. Chouhan, our guide, informed us the Maneri area has developed to be a center for water sports. The lake formed by the dam was a popular venue for boating and other water sports. Where the river cascaded over the steep mountainside, more risky activities, such as riding the rapids, were popular, he informed us. We were surprised. We were on a different mission and such sports seemed totally out of place in relation to our pilgrimage. I personally was glad our pilgrimage did not include plans for boating or riding the rapids.

Gangotri

Finally, after fifty years of waiting and hoping, I was at the place where I could obtain the blessings of *Maa Ganga*, at her origin in the great Himalayas. I prayed that nothing would stop that now. I was glad my family members were with me.

As we approached the Gangotri area, the second stop on the Char Dham pilgrimage, the temperature was falling, and we could feel the difference in the elevation. Thankfully no one in the bus developed any significant difficulty in breathing or other signs of altitude sickness. A couple of us felt slight headaches, but it passed pretty quickly. Although we were reaching heights of ten thousand to eleven thousand feet above sea level, our stops on the way at lower elevations at

Barkot, Yamunotri and at Uttarkashi had helped us to adjust to the thin air at Gangotri.

When we arrived at Gangotri, we gathered our change of clothes for after our bath in the river and proceeded to walk to the river. We made our way down a steep path lined on both sides by shops carrying various pooja items such as brass trays, two-inch high brass lamps, camphor to light in front of the deity and garlands of flowers for us to purchase as offerings to the Goddess at the temple. Even the smallest store had sweet treats, packaged nuts, gift items, and religious artifacts. Navigating our way past all the tempting items, we went straight to the river.

The path to the river was over a mile long. Mountain ranges rose high on either side, many of their tall, angular peaks shining pure white in snow-covered splendor. When I imagined taking a bath at the origins of the river, I did not know how close these white peaks would be, and how cold the air would be. From the river banks I watched the powerful tides of the gushing waters of *Maa Ganga* as she roared down the slopes and over the rocks of the mountain range, and I was rendered speechless because no words could describe the power of the flowing water. Having longed for a dip in the waters of *Maa Ganga* for years, now I was dying to get in.

If Raj was with me he would have made me turn around and leave. There was no way he would let me go into that fast flowing waters where my foothold was uncertain and the air I had to breathe was severely cold. He was very protective of me to the extent it made me crazy sometimes. All his cautionary words resounded in my head. I made a decision that since he was not with me, I had to use my judgment and do what I have to do with more care and forethought than I had done on some previous occasions.

Reaching the water's edge, we had to admit that it would be too dangerous to really submerge ourselves into the cold and fast-flowing waters. The water formed waves around the rocks, and powerful swirls created eddies which I could clearly see that were too strong for us to walk across. We were pre-warned that sudden tides of water may happen in the river because of melting snow from the glacier above. I was disappointed. I was not allowed to go to the center of the river as she rushed downward stream. I would not be immersed in the holy waters, as I had wished at the start of my journey. Rather, I had to be satisfied bathing in the shallow parts of the running current. We saw many rocks on which we could sit while taking a bath by pouring the water onto our bodies. I was frustrated, but I was also resolute. If it was not meant to be that I would not be fully immersed in the river, so be it. I trusted that my Deities had a plan.

The sun was shining bright, yet the air was still freezing cold. We found out that the water temperature was between twenty-five to twenty-seven degrees Fahrenheit. It was not surprising, since just a short while ago the water was part of the Gomukh Glacier, eight miles up the mountain, from where the snow melts to form the origin of the Bhagirathi Ganga, at Gangotri. My small group of pilgrims decided we would take turns to go in the water and that no one would go in alone.

My cousin Usha was to be my buddy. Usha was born the year I turned twelve. We both lived in our *Ammoomma's* house, and her mother, my maternal aunt, was in charge of my education long before Usha was born. In our extended family we were not considered cousins. We were truly sisters. When I left home and came over to the States, she was a young girl, only eleven years old. The next time I saw her she was eighteen years. In the next thirty years we saw each other seven or eight times when I was in Trivandrum on visits that extended three weeks or so at the most. But it did not matter. In matters of the heart, neither distance nor time will diminish the deep connections we make as children. So, it was only natural that she would be looking after me in our adventure in the turbulent parts of this expansive river.

I ventured on to the first rock, and Usha had a stronghold on me to prevent me from going on to the next rock or into deeper waters. She, like my daughters, knew my fervor regarding a bath in the River Ganga, and did not trust my safety instincts at that moment. Sitting on a rock, the water up to my hips, Usha helped to pour the water on me as I took my bath. Even the short bath proved to be extreme as I could feel the freezing waters numb my feet and legs. It took me twelve minutes to finish my bath, and

I was numb all the way up to my knees. Usha helped me out of the river and got me to dry ground. As I thawed out in the bright sun, the cold felt bearable. Maybe it was the warm feeling of having bathed in the Ganges that did it.

I looked up at the clear blue skies above and thanked the Gods up in heaven for my good fortune. Then I offered my thanks to Raj, who I am certain now has a place by Lord Vishnu's side. This is the coveted place to attain when you get to Vaikundom, or Heaven which is Lord Vishnu's abode. My palms brought together in prayer and my head bowed low, I offered my pranams, respectful salutations, to the clear blue waters of the Ganges, sparkling, pure and unadulterated, as she cascaded directly from the glacier at Gomukh peak.

After my bath in her holy waters, I sat by her bank and looked up at the mountain peaks all around. The closer peaks were lush and green with evergreens and flowering trees with white flowers. I was pleasantly surprised at the variety of flora, even at this height of over ten thousand feet. On the taller mountain ranges, the peaks were barren of any greenery, but were adorned by snow caps. I was told that in another four weeks' time, all the areas we now walked upon would be covered by many feet of snow and the temple dedicated to Goddess Ganga would be inaccessible for six months. I had made it just in time before the snows came.

I remembered the writings of the sage Swami Tapovanji, who wandered the Himalayas in the 1930s, and whose writings inspired me to make this journey to Gangotri. In his book Wanderings in the Himalayas, he wrote about the River Ganga emerging from between two rows of high rocks bordered by deodar and other Himalayan trees. "Gangotri is not extensive in area, but in natural beauty it can hold its own against any other spot in the Himalayas," he wrote. "Added to that natural loveliness is its traditional sacredness," he also touted the ancient belief that, "One drop of the water from Ganga would wash away all sins." While I believed that, I also still desired full immersion.

The power I saw in *Maa Ganga*, even her formative descent from the mountains, fully convinced me that she was capable of being the life source for the thousands of people who depend on her waters for their livelihood as she traversed the plains of North India and flowed down elegantly on to the sea at the Bay of Bengal.

As I watched the strong currents flow down the steep mountain, I knew why *Maa Ganga* was so holy and so important to my people. On her course to the Bay of Bengal, the River Ganges merges with Hooghly River in Bengal State. The Howrah Bridge spans over the river in Calcutta. Here the river is very wide, and played a big role in trade with England and other European countries in the past, and still forms a vital path in India's trade. Reaching the Bay of Bengal, the river splits into over two dozen branches, and forms the Ganges delta, before the waters empty into the ocean.

Because this delta is so expansive, it renders a vast area into a very fertile region where crops of rice and other grains, as well as jute are grown, all year round. When I was only eleven years old, I visited Calcutta with my Ammooma. I still remember going over long bridges covering multiple branches of flowing water from the Ganges, and long barges carrying rice grain and jute floating beneath the bridges. At that age, I did not realize how crucial the rivers, and the rains, and the snowmelts were for the daily survival of the people, not only in the local area, but also for all of the rest of the country who depended on the crops and the industries from that area. Later I found out how the trade of such goods from India to the rest of the world, as well as goods reaching India from all parts of the world depended on the water levels of the branches of the River Ganges for timely transportation of such goods via the Indian Ocean.

I changed into dry clothes while the rest of my group took their baths. When they too had changed, we proceed to the temple.

The main temple at Gangotri is dedicated to Goddess Ganga. Marble and silver images of the goddess, decorated in garlands of yellow, white and red flowers, were present within the garba griha, sanctum sanctorum. Around this temple there are also shrines to Lakshmi, goddess of wealth, Saraswathi, Goddess of learning, Annapurna, Goddess of abundance, and Lord Shiva, the God of destruction. In all different forms and with all different names, we Hindus know that it is one God Power that we pray to. Yet, the empowerment we feel after praying in front of a particular deity vary at different times, depending on what stage of our life we are in. At that moment in my life, I felt that praying to the Goddess Ganga was exactly what I needed to do. I prayed that bathing in her holy waters followed by her blessing would lead me to the rebirth of my own spirit, my own sense of self without my beloved other half that I so needed.

As I prayed, my heart was filled with gratitude for having attained the feat of making it up there, especially since I saw the risks the journey posed along the way. I also knew that Goddess Ganga was blessing me in this journey of healing so that I could face my life going forward without my Raj.

But something was still missing. I didn't want to think about it too much, so I prayed that I would find that final peace before this pilgrimage was over.

CHAPTER 4

In Search of Lord Shiva at Kedarnath

September 28, 2011
From Uttarkashi to Srinagar

Having experienced the blessings of *Maa Ganga*, we returned to Uttarkashi. Exhausted from the day trip, I was thankful for a warm meal of chappathis and vegetable curry that awaited us. Once my head hit the pillow, I slept deep and long until we received our usual call for morning coffee. Soon the buckets of hot water arrived. After a refreshing bath, although my body could have used a long hot shower at that point, I joined the others to board the bus to proceed to Srinagar, our next stop on our way to Kedarnath, 238 kilometers or over a hundred miles. Mr. Chouhan led us in chanting "Ganga Devi Ki Jai," victory to Goddess Ganga, and "Ohm NamaShivaya," salutations to the name of Lord Shiva. Shiva is the deity of Kedarnath temple, the third temple in the Char Dham pilgrimage and our next stop.

The bus was bustling with conversation of our experiences at Gangotri. Having shared the road, the food, the rivers and the worship at the temples for five days, the group was now an extended family.

My immediate family called me Paapa Chechi. My pet name at home is Paapa, and Chechi means older sister. Many of the co-pilgrims addressed me as Paapa Chechi, on the first day. I was the oldest member in our group, and by the fifth day I became Maathaji, respected Mother. Some called me "Aunty." I accepted both terms with dignity, and appreciated the love that came with them. Grey hair does have its advantages.

Bathed in the bright sunlight, the mountains looked glorious. I was surprised to see new flowering trees, some similar to those seen in the subtropics, their branches laden with bright yellow flowers blooming in the cold, thirty-degree weather. Scattered on the mountains were tufts of low plants twelve to sixteen inches off the ground, with purplish blue flowers, three inches round, and the leaves were still green.

I remembered my old Yoga teacher, Shirley, talking about them, many years ago. In the eighties on three different occasions, Shirley had stayed with Indian sages in caves in the Himalayan ranges, three to six months at a time. Once the snows were high, the trains stopped running, and the ponies could not carry supplies to the top. They lived on the grains they stored before the snows blocked the roads. For greens in their food, she mentioned that for a few days they could dig through the snow and find some preserved plants. Also, she had described digging up roots of such plants and seeping them in water to make a tea-like drink. She melted snow for water and for cleansing. She described how the grains were stored on ledges carved along the walls of the caves to protect them from mice. The items most at risk were her soap bars from America, which the mice would eat if they got their paws on them. It was a constant source of laughter in our yoga groups when she mentioned that. I was not going to stay in any such caves. Our group had pretty decent accommodations at the end of the day in hotels or rest-houses.

While I was focused on my mission to find spiritual renewal, I couldn't help but be interested in knowing the history and geography of the places we journeyed through. India's culture is thousands of years old, with religion melding into history and geography. I was curious to know why subtropical plants flourished in the high, cold Himalayas. I discovered that plate-tectonics explain their presence. Approximately twenty million years ago, India was connected to the southeastern tip of Africa. Stresses in the earth's crust resulted in the development of a rift between them. India broke free and began drifting north as part of the Indo-Australian Plate. The leading edge of the plate was oceanic crust. Several millions of years later this leading oceanic edge collided with the Eurasian Plate and began to be thrust upward. India slammed into Asia, and eventually, the deep sea-floor of the Indo-Australian Plate rose above sea level, and the Himalayas were born. Today, India continues its push northward. The Himalayas, once the deep sea-floors of an ancient sea, are now a majestic terrestrial mountain range. The geologists were surprised when they discovered the fossilized remains of ancient sea creatures at the top of the world.

I also learned that the Garhwal Himalayas were steeped in religious history. The silver mountains, the sparkling streams, vivid green valleys and the cool climate have attracted many into the hills of Garhwal for peace, tranquility and meditation. It is this beautiful land that inspired the great poet and sage Maharishi Valmiki. Sage Valmiki is celebrated as the poet harbinger in Sanskrit literature. He wrote the epic Ramayana, the story of the incarnation of Lord Rama, in Sanskrit.

All this laid the ultimate foundation for the literary treasures of Garhwal, works of art and famous paintings. Being that the focus of this trip was my pilgrimage to *Maa Ganga*, and the temples situated at the origins of her tributaries, I could not pursue the side trips to visit the paintings, stone carvings, and wood carvings for which the Garhwal region is famous for. Still, I consider myself really blessed to have walked the mountains where such holy men had roamed and to have experienced the peace and beauty of this sacred land.

Our next stop was Srinagar, the capital of the Garhwal Kingdom in the sixteenth century. It is a very important cultural and educational center. Being placed in central Garhwal at a moderate height, it is an important Valley Bazar in the hills.

At dusk we reached Srinagar and settled down, knowing the next day was also going to be a long trip to get to Kedarnath.

September 29—Srinagar to Kedarnath

Having achieved the goal of my pilgrimage to *Maa Ganga* at Gangotri, even though my bath in the river was not a full immersion, I was more relaxed and my mind was fully open to the new experiences I knew awaited me on the remainder of the trip.

We started early from Srinagar so we could get to Kedarnath early enough in the day to fully experience the great temple there. Kedarnath temple is dedicated to Lord Shiva, who as the mystic yogi meditated in serene solitude in the Kedar hills.

Since time immemorial, this shrine remains perched on a mountain ridge in this remote part of the Garhwal Himalayas, hewn from the granite of the mountains surrounding it. In ancient times, the area was so inaccessible that it was said that at Kedarnath "one finds oneself almost at the threshold of eternity."

On this day, seeing that my trip was towards a temple in honor of Lord Shiva at Kedarnath, the prayers I chanted were to Lord Shiva.

Lord Shiva is Shakti or power; Shiva is the Destroyer, the most powerful god of the Hindu pantheon and one of the godheads in the Hindu Trinity. Unlike the godhead Brahma, the Creator, or Vishnu, the Preserver, Shiva is believed to be at the core of the centrifugal force of the universe because of his responsibility for death and destruction. Shiva is the dissolving force in life, but many misunderstand what that means and the power inherent in destruction. Destruction is not always bad, for it is the necessary step towards its opposite, construction—birth or rebirth. Thus Shiva dissolves in order to create, since death is the medium for rebirth into a new life. So the opposites of life and death and creation and destruction both reside in his character.

In temples, the deity of Shiva is usually represented as a phallic symbol, called the linga, which represents the energies necessary for life on both the microcosmic and the macrocosmic levels—in other words, the world in which we live and the world which constitutes the whole of the universe.

The actual image of Shiva is also distinct from other deities: his hair is always piled high on the top of his head with a crescent moon adorning it. A stream of water representing the river Ganges is shown tumbling down from his hairs. Around his neck is a coiled serpent representing Kundalini or the spiritual energy within life. He holds a trident in his left hand in which is bound the damroo (small leather drum). He sits on a tiger skin and on his right is a water pot. He wears Rudraksha beads and his whole body is smeared with ash, believed to be from the cremation grounds where he roams.

The Kedarnath Temple, one of the twelve holiest temple sites in India, is mentioned in the epic story of Mahabharatha (400 AD – 700 AD). In that epic, a major family conflict among the Kauravas and their cousins, the Pandavas, lead to a war at Kurukshetra. The Pandavas with the help of Lord Krishna defeat the Kaurava cousins. Although they win the war, the sadness and remorse of being the cause for the demise of their cousins, uncles, and other family members who fought on the Kaurava side, is overwhelming. The five Pandava princes are ready to give up the hard-won kingdom, but Lord Krishna convinces them to do their duty on earth. They rule the kingdom but with a dispassionate detachment.

A few years later, they hand over their kingdom to their heirs, and the five princes travel up to the Himalayas. Reaching the Swargarohana Peaks, the snow-topped mountains just above the Kedar hills, they prepare to end their mortal lives to ascend to the heavenly abode. In the Kedar hills, they pray to Lord Shiva. After ardent efforts with intense and persistent prayers from the Pandavas, Lord Shiva appears before them. He listened to their prayers of atonement for their part in the war at Kurukshetra and absolved them of their guilt. Grateful for his services, the Pandavas build a temple at Kedarnath in honor of Lord Shiva. They used blocks of hard rock from the mountainside, and the grey façade of the temple still merges with the mountain peaks in graceful harmony.

Pilgrims have been travelling to Kedarnath since the first and most famous pilgrim, Sri Sankaracharya, also known as Adi Sankara, travelled to the site in 788 A.D. Pilgrims have thus been the earliest writers of history says Srimathi Subhadra Sen Gupta, in her book, The Dhaams of the Himalayas. It was the pilgrims travelling across India to these very remote and often dangerous places who would record their journeys, which included cultural and geographic history.

Adi Sankara was born in the State of Kerala in South India, and at the very young age of eleven years, he left home and travelled all over India spreading the principles of Sanatana Dharma. Sanatana Dharma is the original name of what is now popularly called Hinduism or Hindu Dharma. The terms Hindu and Hinduism are more recent developments. Sanatana Dharma, or Hinduism, is a code of ethics, a way of living through which one may achieve moksha (enlightenment or liberation). It is the world's most ancient culture and the social, spiritual, and religious tradition of almost one billion of the earth's inhabitants. Sanatana Dharma represents much more than just a religion; rather, it provides its followers with an entire worldview, of a way of life with a coherent and rational view of reality.

Sage Adi Sankara visited the Kedarnath temple in the ninth century, restored the temple, and established regular pooja services April through October when the temple was accessible. During the snow-covered winter months the worship of Kedarnath is conducted at the Shiva temple in the town of Ukhinath at a much lower and more accessible altitude of 5,400 feet.

He started a pilgrimage on foot from Rameswaram, an island town along the southeast coast of India, travelled to the very southern tip to Kanyakumai, and going up to middle India on to the west and proceeding all the way north to the Himalayan ranges. In the caves of the freezing cold mountains, he lived and meditated and made it his mission to eliminate erratic, unclear, and uncouth elements within the Hindu religious practices.

Although many sages lived and prayed in the Himalayas, Adi Sankara was the one who travelled the most all over India, and was the one Sage who unified the practice of Hinduism throughout the land. He also formulated guidelines and unified the pooja services in the various parts of India. His drastic measures are credited for the true revival of Hinduism and the survival of Hinduism as we see it practiced today, all over the world.

When he reached Kedarnath, Adi Sankara was upset to see how run down the temple was. He restored the temple at Kedarnath and bringing experienced priests from South India (my region), revived religious practices and established regular pooja services. He was the most vocal of the holy men, and he gave new life to the temples in the mountains, especially the one at Badrinath. History has shown that sometime in the past the Vishnu Temple had changed and a Buddhist temple had taken its place. Adi Sankara re-established idol of Vishnu at Badrinath. He also put in place the custom that the main priest, called Ravalji, had to come from our south Indian state of Kerala, Adi Sankara's home State.

Adi Sankara strengthened the rituals not just at the main temples for Shiva but the four main temples for Lord Vishnu in the four corners of India, starting with the temple at Badrinath in the North (the one I was to visit next after Kedarnath), Dwaraka in the West, Puri at the East, and the Rameswaram temple in South India. It is a well-known fact that Sri Adi Sankara's journey always started at the temple in Rameswaram and that he walked his way around India three times to strengthen the bonds and rituals practiced all around the land.

I had known much of this history of Adi Sankara since my youth, and I was truly excited to visit this most holy temple devoted to Lord Shiva at Kedernath. My devotion to Lord Shiva goes back a long time. Starting in 1963 when I married Raj, I had performed a special fast every Monday in honor of Shiva. The Thinkalaksha Vratham, or Monday fast, was a ritual that many women undertook as a specific offering to keep the man of the house healthy and to promote his standing in the world. I grew up believing that if the man of the house was well and happy, the rest of the family will also be happy and the home life harmonious.

Every Monday morning I took a bath, lit the oil lamp in front of Lord Shiva's idol, and said my prayers even before I made a cup of coffee. I ate only vegetarian food for the entire day. Breakfast was fruits and coffee, lunch usually oats porridge or just a hot chocolate with a banana, and the only solid meal was supper, after the evening prayers. That too was only vegetarian foods. In our younger days, no meat was ever served at my dinner table on Mondays. Later on, even if I had to serve meat on Mondays, I myself did not cook it or eat it on that special day. Not only was it a healthy practice to avoid meat once a week, my religious beliefs did not make me blind to the fact that there were too many factors that are not under my control and that we had to endure whatever life offered us.

This particular Monday custom of prayers, including the fast, is believed to be one of the most effective prayer rituals, because it is patterned after a long and rigorous fast that Goddess Parvathi undertook to win over Lord Shiva to marry her.

Parvathi was the daughter of King Himavat, the king of the Himalaya Mountains. She fell in love with Lord Shiva while he meditated in the mountains as an ascetic. The difficulty lay in the fact that at the time, Lord Shiva was standing in a yogic pose, on one leg, atop a Himalayan peak, eyes closed and mind shut off from the rest of the world. So to have broken this intense meditative state and bring him back to living status was by no means a simple task. Parvathi's celestial beauty was legendary but her devotion and dedicated service to the ascetic Shiva did not help to win his affection. She decided to win Shiva's love with prayer and penance. She stayed in the forest and did severe penance, rejecting all comforts of home, and even fasting for days at a time, spending all the hours praying to Shiva. Eventually her efforts were fruitful and Lord Shiva broke his ascetic way of life and married her.

Because Parvathi Devi accomplished this by her long fast, undaunted by many obstacles, this is considered the fast to take for a bright future for any girl. After marriage, many women continue the fast, as I did, believing that the health and mental status of the "man of the house" was most crucial factor in maintaining the stability of any house and home.

Devi Parvathi is now considered the lineal progenitor of all other Goddesses. She is worshipped in different forms and names. Durga is a demon fighting form which she took to kill the Demon Durgam. Lalita means she who plays, and she plays with the Universe as if it is her big toy.

As an adult I have pondered why and how my knowledge of the Hindu pantheon the epic stories and the powers attributed to the Gods and Goddesses have influenced my life in this modern world, particularly in the United States. Fully believing that the power of the Divine within me is part of the God power in the Universe has helped me in all aspects of my life. Leading a hectic life, taking the responsibilities of being a doctor, running a laboratory, and raising a family would have been insurmountable without the confidence my Hindu ideologies gave me. It was my

Karma to do and experience all of it, and my Dharma to get it done in this lifetime.

The bus route to Kedarnath followed the river Mandakini, another main tributary of the River Ganga. Some of the mountains peaks looked similar to ones I saw on my way to Gangotri. The higher we went the more I saw masses of dazzling snow to the north and west. In areas where the snow melted, the mountains looked black or red, the bare rocks shining glossy in the bright sunlight reflected from the dazzling snow. At 12,000 ft. and higher, many of the mountain-sides and peaks shone silver because of snow cover.

As our bus approached the drop-off point leading up to the temple at Kedarnath, I saw the grandeur in the mountains. Combined with the dark grey granite temple and the freezing cold weather, I felt a mesmerizing divineness and spirituality in a landscape full of beauty, peace, and holiness. Small streams flowing from between the rocky slopes appeared unimpressive until they joined to form the Mandakini River. Farther down, the Mandakini River converges with the other tributaries to form the mighty Ganga, The Ganges River.

The sun's rays held no warmth. But the sight of the mountain peaks! Pointing straight up to the heavens, some peaks snow-covered and pure white, others still topped by evergreens, and yet others above the green line showing jagged edges of grey and black stone at the top, looking like polished granite.

The bus took us around hairpin curves, up the side of one mountain, and then downhill to the next valley before we traversed the next mountain. Sometimes the distance from one temple to the other was only twenty-five miles as the crow flies, but to go across two mountain peaks to get to the next destination it was a trip of over 160 miles. I thanked God we were in good hands with the experienced driver and helper on this trip to the Himalayas.

Kedarnath Temple

Once the bus dropped us off, we were told that reaching to the Kedarnath Temple would the biggest challenge of our entire pilgrimage. This information was more than a little daunting—the bus ride up to the temple drop off was harrowing enough in itself. Now we were aiming to reach the highest point of our trip. A steep path, seven miles long lay ahead of us, and it was going to be arduous.

We had a few choices of transport. You could ride up in a doli, a seat mounted on two long bamboo poles and carried up by four young men atop their shoulders. Not everybody wished to be carried up in a doli. Barring heavy, dark clouds, windstorms, and thunderstorms a few helicopters were available to get up there. A few pilgrims did go towards the helipad. The rest of us travelled to the bus park and chose to ride a pony, walk the distance, or be taken up in a doli.

I chose a doli ride. After being bumped up and down in the doli for about two miles, I descended, and decided to walk for a while. Amal, one of the four carriers, walked with me. It was slow and seemed to take forever. The other three rested and then caught up with us at a roadside dabba. I only walked about a mile before I resumed my ride. The bumpy doli was preferable to negotiating the steep incline and rocky trail.

Suddenly the sun disappeared behind clouds and dark dense fog rolled in wave after wave, covering the plants and treetops and making it difficult to even see the edge of our walking path. The only saving grace was the fence at the edge of the path, painted in red, white and green, the colors of the Indian flag. That helped keep my spirits up, but little else could. I was too consumed with surviving the present moment to think about much of anything else. Our guides weren't joking when they said this was difficult.

About an hour later as we carefully and slowly ascended the mountain, the fog lifted and disappeared as quickly as it had arrived. The sun came out and our mood lifted, just as the fog had.

Finally, we reached the village just below the temple. My cousins who rode up on ponies were ready and waiting for me to start up the next trek up to the temple itself. Quickly dropping off my meager possessions at a rest-house, I joined them. It was freezing cold despite sweaters and jackets.

We reached the temple at last. We had started our trek to the temple early in the morning and it was now dusk—a testimony to the difficulty of those seven miles.

Framed in the rear by snow laden peaks of the Swargarohana Mountains, the granite blocks of the Kedarnath temple truly did blend with the peace and calm of the mountain-side. Many pilgrims from all walks of life stood in long lines to reach the sanctum in order to see Lord Shiva, the main deity at this temple.

The crowds were impolite, the weather cold, and I was tired. Looking back, it really was an amazing feat. The temple is extremely difficult to access, yet people were there by the hundreds—and hundreds would come every day to pray and worship at this most sacred shrine to Shiva. The fervor with which I moved along in the line awaiting a darshan, the revered sight of the Shiva prathishta, which means "installed deity," made me forget all physical and mental tiredness.

I was up with the youngest and strongest amid us, pushing forward to see the idol of Lord Shiva. It felt surreal, moving along with the tide of the pilgrims' bodies, not really walking. Then, all of a sudden I was in front of Lord Shiva.

Here, the deity was not in the usual form of the Lord in a seated pose with his hair up and his trident by his side. Neither was it upright lingam, or phallic form of the Shiva Force. Here he was represented as a rock form, sort of curved and slightly lifted at one half, a hump-shaped idol.

The story goes that when the Pandavas of Mahabharata fame (the princes I mentioned in the previous journal entry) came to get Shiva's blessings, he, Lord Shiva played a trick on them. He took the form of Nandi, his bull, and spread himself out over the peaks in the Himalayas, thus making it difficult for the princes to recognize him. However, Bheema detected parts of Shiva, and caught him by Nandi's tail. It was ultimately over the hump of the Nandi-Bull form of Shiva that the main temple at Kedarnath was built.

That was what I was now seeing, the rock-form now covered by all the special pooja offerings. Chandanam, or sandalwood paste, and Kumkumam, the red powder used to adorn the deity, and all the flowers placed on the deity by pilgrims ahead of us. I could only savor a few moments in the front of Shiva. I got pushed forward in line, so others could view him.

It was also interesting but discomforting to see army personnel carrying guns escorting us pilgrims up and around the temple. This was necessary because we were not far from the Tibetan border, which is of course occupied by the Chinese, and the area was politically unstable.

Walking out of the main temple, I did three pradikshans, circumambulations, around the temple, including the statue of Nandi, Lord Shiva's bull, who sits in the outer courtyard facing the Shiva's inner sanctum.

However, the most beautiful and one of the most memorable parts of my entire journey happened as we approached the temple for the first time. As I noted, it was dusk when we arrived, just in time for the Sringar

Darshan, a beautiful sight. That is how the evening pooja services are described.

The main priest was escorted into the Sanctum sanctorum to the accompaniment of drum beats and saxophone music. A bell ringer stood ready beneath the huge bell. He held the rope that hung from it, waiting for the sign from the musicians. For this evening service, the deity is bedecked with flowers and gold ornaments and a golden umbrella suspended from above. Lit by the glow of the burning camphor and the lamps at the time of the aarti, it is considered a great blessing to be able to view the deity at this special time. The devotees congregated by the door to catch a glimpse of the form of Shiva during the aarti. The inner temple space was too crowded and we were forced to attend the pooja services from the outside courtyard.

I stood there in the eerie twilight, bathed in the glow emanating from the wicks of the flickering flames of a thousand oil lamps lit along and around the four walls of the temple. The atmosphere was thick with the intense aroma of incense smoke arising from the mist at every corner. Accompanied by loud chanting of Sanskrit slokas, Vedic prayers, by four or five priests, the main priest, the poojari, offered flower petals over the idol. He repeatedly waved the oil lamp holding about thirty or forty lit wicks over the idol, the flames reflecting on the gold ornaments placed on Shiva's idol. Suddenly the tempo of the drumbeats and the saxophones increased; the bell-ringer picked up on the cue and started ringing the bell, hanging on to the bell rope for dear life as he swung back and forth. The air was split open by the voluble sounds of the bells. It was amazing that I, who grew up in the sea-level town of Trivandrum, was listening to the prayer bells at a mountain top temple dedicated to the Lord Shiva at twelve thousand feet above sea level.

The loud clanging of the temple bell throughout the ceremony resounded in the still cold air of the mountains for what seemed to be over five minutes. This gave me an opportunity to telephone Shanthi, my sister in Trivandrum, and enabled her to listen to them. My daughters in the United States came next. Devi answered the phone. It was a precious moment of connection as I had her listen to the loud ringing of the bells at Kedarnath at aarti. Neither she nor I could digest the significance at the moment. Then I dialed Nimmi. She too heard the bells. The next call to Molly was answered by her answering machine. I still don't know how I had the presence of mind to let the machine record the bells for Molly. I did. When I tried to call Sandhya, my niece who lives right behind my house to let her listen, it was too late. The bells had ended.

I have always proclaimed that no human contact is ever for nothing. Before I left Chicago to go on this pilgrimage I read my friend Uma's account of her trip to Char Dham in 2008, and it had stuck in my mind how she had called her relatives in South India during worship at Kedarnath to listen to the same prayer bells. I am glad I remembered.

The aarti had ended, and the bells stopped. The rarity of the air at that height, combined with the strident clanging of the evening bells and the clamorous chanting of prayers by hundreds of devotees put me in a state of unadulterated ecstasy. When my breathing came back to normal, I realized how breathless I was the whole time of the aarti. The bells, the altitude and my fervor had me on a high that I had never experienced before in my entire life.

Growing up we were told that the bells during any pooja services invoked a special sound within us, a vibration that raised our inner awareness to a special height. We were also taught that the sounds of the bells carried our prayers and intentions beyond the earth on to the universe, to invite divine help in all the things we did. Later I have also learned that the sound of the bells suppressed any other distractions around us while we prayed during aarti and pooja functions. To hear the sounds of the bells from the special Shiva temple in the high Himalayas adds a new level of blessing for us.

When the services were over and the mountain-side quieter, my eyes were closed in prayer and I am not certain how long it took me to come back to earth. I could not believe my good fortune to enable my family to listen to the sacred sounds of an evening aarti at Kedarnath Temple, a towering twelve thousand feet up in the Himalayas. I had really sent the blessed sounds of those prayer bells all the way across more than ten thousand miles to a place three continents away. To be not only blessed with the experience, but also to be able to share the poignant moments with loved ones sent a shiver down my whole being. I looked up to the snow-clad peaks which I saw as the closest to heaven I could be at that point, and sent a silent thanks heavenward. I thanked God that no snow storms prevented my trip to reach Lord Shiva at Kedarnath.

Ohm Namashivaya! (Ohm, salutations and adoration to the name of Shiva.)

That night, I went to bed fully clothed, including my North Face trek-jacket my son-in-law had insisted on buying me for this trip, and covered by two of the extra thick lambs-wool blankets provided by the hotel. I still shivered and finally fell asleep from sheer exhaustion. It was below the freezing point, twenty-six degrees Fahrenheit. The hotel had no central heating, and portable heaters were not allowed because of safety risks.

Next morning, around 4:00 a.m. I woke up to a hot cup of coffee as usual, thanks to our diligent cooks. I was supplied with boiling hot water in buckets to mix with the cold water from the tap, for an early bath before I went to the temple. At 5:00 a.m. my party of seven walked back to the temple, a good mile distance from the hotel. My teeth chattered, despite wearing a warm sweater and a jacket. I said an extra prayer to Lord Shiva to keep me safe and not fall ill by the end of the day. Under the guidance of a priest I did a special

Nirvana Pooja, special offerings for enlightenment, to Lord Shiva.

In the South Indian temples, we are not allowed to step within the sanctum sanctorum where the deity is ensconced. Only the designated priests go inside to perform the prescribed pooja rituals as our representatives and according to Vedic rituals. We, the devotees, stay just outside the door to the sanctum, and when the pooja is over, the offerings of flowers, the sandalwood paste which decorated the idols, and the food we had offered are distributed to the devotees as prasadams, meaning blessed items.

There are twelve such idols of Shiva, called Jyothirlingams in India. Jyoti means "radiance" and lingam the "mark or sign" of Shiva. It is believed that a person can see these lingas as columns of fire piercing through the earth after he reaches a higher level of spiritual attainment. As a result of my journey to the mountains to bathe in the pure waters of *Maa Ganga*, I was rewarded with the opportunity to do my humble prostrations at the feet of the highest Jyothirlingam at Kedarnath. I had already worshipped at the Jyothirlingam in Varanasi, Benares, when I was eleven years old, in 1951.

When I went to Varanasi as a child, I was shocked to see all devotees were allowed to offer the flowers directly on to the idols that represented the deity in the sanctum. I objected to the practice of doing the service directly on the idol, and I protested that the sanctity was ruined by the people in North India by touching the idol during worship.

Now, older and wiser, I followed the lead of the other pilgrims and made contact with the three sided rock which formed the idol of Lord Shiva at Kedarnath. I was surprised that now I had no qualms about offering libations of water, milk and ghee (melted, clarified butter), directly onto the idol, and placing flowers personally, directly, onto the idol of Lord Shiva.

When I was eleven, and truthfully through most of my life, I did not ever dream that I would breathe the air at the highest temple for Lord Shiva at Kedarnath. I had come a long way. By this time in my life I had realized that the physical rituals, although a definite part of our prayer services, were not the true essence of my prayers, and that it was not really my physical body that accepted the divine solace provided from the powers above. The spiritual being that I am, connected to the divine powers invoked by the prayer rituals, thus empowering my whole being to enjoy the fruits of the experience. At eleven years of age, I was too young to have known this. At seventy-one, although I cannot claim to have realized all the secrets of the Universe, I had experienced enough of the divine gifts to recognize the truth of the matter. I felt a glow of accomplishment as I completed the pooja and walked outside. I knew my Ammoomma was smiling at me from the heavens.

As I finished my rituals, I also realized that each time I have visited a temple of Shiva's Jyothirlingam,

I have reaped tangible benefits. As a youngster, even at my early age of eleven, I had felt a power rising within me that helped solidify my passion for a career in medicine. It was as if I was elevated a step closer to attain what I wished in life.

As I stood looking at the magnificent Kedarnath temple, I felt more able to accept my loss. It had been ten months since my husband Raj passed away. Despite all his health problems, Raj was with me for fifteen years after his liver transplant. At Kedarnath, I was able to do my pranams at the feet of Lord Shiva and say thanks for all the additional time I had with my sweetheart. With Raj gone, as I floundered to find the best path forward in my life, I felt honored to lay all my cares and worries about my survival without Raj at the feet of Lord Shiva. It gave me solace that I could still depend on Lord Shiva to make things happen. I felt confident that I can still achieve many great things in life knowing that Lord Shiva's blessings are with me and that Raj's love will always be with me even if he is not within my sight.

I walked over to a memorial hall, adjacent to the Shiva temple, to the site where the Sage Sankaracharya had undergone Samadhi, attainment of salvation at death. Along with the pilgrims in my group, I sat on the stone floor in meditation. As I drew in the calm but uplifting energy from the serene and cold air, I wished I had planned this trip a long time ago. Yet, I knew deep in my heart that my getting there at this time happened when it was meant to be. At the completion of a deep, long, and gratifying meditation session, I walked out into bright sunshine, and came face to face with the Swargarohana peaks, which is where the Pandavas were last seen, before they ascended to heaven.

Maybe this is where my dear Raj also passed on to his heavenly abode.

Descending from the mountain, I was carried down in a doli by the four young men. When I first accepted the ride, I imagined I would feel like Cleopatra riding in style. Once I was lifted aloft the doli, I didn't feel so regal. Yet, knowing these four young people made a living for six months of the year doing this job, I had no guilt in taking the ride. On the other hand, after conversing with them in their minimal English and my minimal Hindi, I gathered how important the job was to each of them

Already late September, their present jobs would end in five weeks when the November snowfall in this part of the mountain would force closing the temple. One of them, Thakur, was returning to Nepal and going back to school for six months. Two others would travel two and a half days to Delhi or towns near Delhi to find jobs until the mountains were accessible again next April or May. So, what money they earned now, including the tips, had to tide them until the next spring when they could find work again in the mountains.

They were a jolly bunch. Each time I decided to trek the path, Amal accompanied me to carry my bag. With my camera, my daily meds, telephone, Oats and Honey nutrition bars, and sugar pills to avoid hypoglycemia, the shoulder bag was heavier than I intended. But knowing I couldn't reach our camp for hours at a time, I was well-prepared for the trek up to the temple and back to our base camp. I walked down for a mile and a half distance, and waited for the remaining three to bring down the doli. Amal even took pictures of me with the mountains in the background. I was blessed to meet such hard-working young people.

September 30, 2011
Kedarnath to Guptkashi, on the way to Badrinath

The trip down the mountain from the Kedarnath temple was even more daunting than the trip up because the steep mountainside was hard to walk without losing balance in many spots. But when I calmed down and got into the rhythm of the walk, I felt surefooted and unafraid. I knew it was because of the strength I found from my prayers at Kedarnath. Although I had not quite gotten to a point of being completely certain that I can go on alone without my dear Raj, at least I was getting comfortable in this journey I was taking.

At the beginning of the path the mountains were rocky, with only some short scrubby plants about a foot tall and a foot around. A few green leafy plants with sparse yellow flowers about an inch in diameter dotted the landscape. The rocks shone bright, black, or grey depending on the angle of the sunlight hitting them.

An occasional waterfall dropped precipitously down the mountainside. On two occasions within the seven mile distance the water flowed over the path we were on, splashing us and our ponies. Many of the pilgrims and a few of the ponies stopped to drink from the fresh sparkling water flowing down the rocks.

Far to my left, I saw a rivulet of water, which as we descended, became larger and larger, with the many waterfalls merging into it. As I walked down, or was carried down in the doli, my path got closer to this particular stream, and by the time I came down from twelve thousand feet to nine thousand feet, it was a gurgling, rolling river, the Mandakini tributary of the mighty Ganga.

It had taken a shining silvery appearance as it gushed down the rocky slopes. I was awed to see the transformation and the power of a river being born. The scrubby vegetation was gone. The slopes and the riverbanks had taken on a deep green hue, with green leafy bushes, about three to four feet tall. Farther down, firs and other variety of tall evergreens appeared, giving a different majesty to the mountains.

I was starting to wonder why I had not seen any birds at the very top. An hour later, and down my path, crow-like black and grey colored birds, but half the size of crows and not as loud or boisterous, appeared. They flitted around the roadside dabha eating of the food dropped by pilgrims and drinking from puddles forming by the water taps. Dogs were everywhere. In the higher slopes I saw dogs bearing thick coats resembling a lamb's wool coat and manes as wide as you would see in young lions. They had bushy tails and were the size of large German shepherds.

After my return I found out these are Tibetan Mastiffs, also called Mountain dogs. At a lower altitude, sheepdogs appeared, singly and as twosome or three, but they didn't appear to be guarding any sheep, goats or cattle. It was like they were drifters. A few birds, the size of small hens, appeared among the trees, touting dark blue shiny feathers. Some of these did fly as high as maybe forty or fifty feet, reaching up to the lower branches of the fir trees. They kept to the shade and they hid well among the thick branches of the trees, making it impossible for me to get a photograph. I did not get a good sighting to get details on their caps to identify them later.

Suddenly, two hawks appeared soaring above tree tops in their regal swoops without flapping a wing, gliding smooth and high up in the air. They were elegant but gave me the eerie feeling they were watching me from above.

I boarded the bus again. When the bus got too close to the edge of the road, it took all my willpower to not look down at the precipitous drops of the mountain-side and on to the river gorge deep down below me. Going up the mountain seemed dangerous enough but the trip down was downright terrifying. I knew people died going up and down these mountain passes, but I forced myself to keep my eyes on the mountain tops. I resisted the urge to look too close to where the bus was. It reminded me that in our lives we need to be aware of dangers, and take precautions, but it should not stop our actions. If the threat of danger paralyzes us, we will be stuck in places and predicaments we cannot escape. To retract from such situations will only create steeper mountains to climb as we put ourselves in more and deeper danger.

Another two thousand feet down, vast apple orchards bearing red apples and some with mixed gold and red fruit and even a few gatherings of pear trees appeared. At the next town we stopped for lunch, the stores carried apples and pears in abundance. It was interesting to see the reaction of the pilgrims from the south who saw pears for the first time in their lives. The similarity to a fruit called Sabargilli, which we grew in the south of India, was remarkable, yet the tastes were not quite the same. They were fascinated to hear how I had grown pears in my backyard. I shared my story with them.

In the seventies, in the U.S., Raj and I grew a home orchard. Four apple trees, two pears, three plums, two peaches, and two cherry trees. It took a great deal of physical labor and much of our free time between our busy medical practice and childrearing to tend to our orchard. The children helped shop for the trees when we first planted them. It was a novel experience and holds one of my fondest memories of my children. We came across a pear tree which was crooked and sad looking. Raj and I looked at it but passed it by. My eight year old daughter, Devi, was in tears. "No one will buy the poor crooked one if we don't," she stuttered between sobs. Raj laughed. I shook my head. So we bought the crooked little pear tree, planted it in our yard and gave it some extra TLC. It rewarded us with many delicious pears for years to come.

Every fall we gathered the fruit from our orchard, shared with family and friends, and had plenty left over for the local food pantry. I close my eyes and I see Raj chasing our German Shepherd with an apple in hand scaring the wits out of the poor dog at apple picking time.

As I looked out the window, terraced farming graced by fields of rice appeared. A few farmhouses were scattered among the extensive farms. This reminded me of the vast rice paddies in Trivandrum on flat land, which were totally different from the terracing that was needed on the mountain slopes to hold water at the roots of the rice plants. Some of the farms still had ripe rice fields glowing golden in the sunshine, while others were in different stages of harvest. Boys and men walking behind plows drawn by oxen were scattered within my view. Many farms showed bare earth, with bundles of hay dotting the landscape of the harvested fields. Women wearing bright red, green and brown colored clothes were busy forking the hay before the bales were rolled or stacked in the fields.

Scattered along the roadside were numerous storage sheds, with roll-up doors that looked like garage doors. The name Basmati was painted in large letters on these doors. Basmati rice is a very aromatic grain with a distinct taste which is almost twice as long as most other rice grains. It is favored in the making of Biriyani, a fried-rice dish flavored with saffron and cardamom, and to which curried meat or vegetables are added. Biriyani makes a very wholesome dish when supplemented with yogurt and tomatoes, as long as the amount of butter added is kept to a minimum. I smiled when we came upon a town named Basmati. Not too subtle but it underscored the importance of the crop for the region.

As had been the case for the past eight days, the bus route intertwined with the course of the River Ganga, a full force of nature by now, exhilarating, and quite intimidating.

Even in the midst of the twenty co-pilgrims, I was often alone with my thoughts.

"Some people are born happy," says the Celtic Scholar John O'Donohue. I know I am one of them. In our younger days, Raj and I had arguments, often loud, but at the end, I remember being thankful that we were so passionate about our interests. For this, and a few other attitudes I touted, my daughters have called me a cockeyed optimist. Just recently my neurologist told me that my tests showed severe Carpal tunnel changes on both my wrists, and that I had a right to complain about more pain. I laughed. I really did not have more pain than I claimed.

I remember being genuinely sad only on a few occasions in the past, when my Dad passed away in 1970, when my Mom, my Ammachi, and my Ammoomma, died in the 80s and 90s. I was not sad just because they had left this world. I could accept the fact that it was time for them to go. But I was sad because I was unable to be with them in their last days to tend to them or make them happy with my presence beside them.

Nine months after Raj died, I felt more sadness than I had ever felt. It was more than just mourning his departure. It came in waves especially in late mornings at the hours when I used to tend to his needs. There was a space which I could not fill in spite of all the physical and social activities I tried. I felt like a truck with one wheel stuck in the mud, reeling around in one place. I wondered if mourning of any form for too long a period would really help anyone find their path to a new life when their dear one is not with them anymore.

I knew I had to overcome this feeling to be able to go forward with my family and my writing. I planned this pilgrimage to do just that, get me on track and help find my momentum. Having completed the second phase of my pilgrimage, and despite the obvious dangers, I knew I was in a better mental state, able to enjoy the majesty of the mountains and the changing landscape rendered possible by the power of the water coming down from their heights. I knew enough to know that I could be happy with the energy I had gained at Kedarnath, but a part of me still wanted more. We had two more sites to visit, and I wondered what awaited me there.

Fig. 1: Shaku weds Raj, January 21, 1963

Fig. 2: Raj and Shaku at Kanyakumari, January 12th, 2006

Fig. 3: My niece, Radhika, holding me after Raj's ashes are immersed in the ocean, January 24th, 2011.

△ **Trivandrum:** My hometown, where I lived until I was 23 years old.

✳ **Delhi:** *My Pilgrimage to Maa Ganga* in Uttarkhand in 2011 started from Delhi.

The red area in the small insert is Uttrakhand.

Fig. 4: The map has been sourced from MapsofIndia.com with due permission.

Fig. 5: A priest performs an *"Aarti,"* a special blessing, of our bus before the start of our journey.

Fig. 6: The Himalayan ranges appear at a distance.

Fig. 7: My family, Vatsala, Gautam, Sasibhooshan, Bindu, Susheela and Usha.

Fig. 8: Shaku gets blessings from the holy waters of Maa Ganga.

Fig. 9: Shaku by Maa Ganga, at Rishikesh.

Fig. 10: Shivananda Ashram

Fig. 11: Lakshman Jhula, a 480 feet suspension bridge over the River Ganga, at Rishikesh.

Fig. 12: Shaku and family crossing Ganga on Lekshman Jhula, the suspension bridge.

Fig. 13: Water sports on the wide, fast flowing river at Rishikesh

Fig. 14: Sunrise through the Cedars.

Fig. 15: A roadside dabba overlooking the mountains.

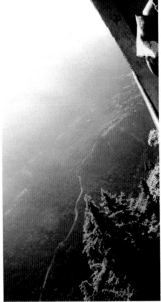

Fig. 17: Shaku on a bridge over the River Yamuna.

Fig. 16: A roadside dabba, with the river seen deep below.

Fig. 18: Shaku riding on Anjali the pony.

Fig. 20: Mustard fields in the mountains. The field shows partial harvest.

Fig. 19: Yamunotri Temple.

Fig. 21: Mustard fields in the mountains.

Fig. 22: Ganga aarti.

Fig. 23: Shaku performing Ganga aarti.

Fig. 24 & 25: Bhagirathi Ganga as it flows from Gomukh peak.

Fig. 26: Shaku and Usha (both in red) in the waters of the Bhagirathi Ganga.

Fig. 27: A closer view of Shaku and Usha in the waters of the Bhagirathi Ganga.

Fig. 28: Hands folded in prayer;
Shaku offers thanks for Maa Ganga's
blessings.

Fig. 29a: Shaku at Gangotri Temple

Fig. 29: My family in front of Gangotri Temple. My nephew
Gautam, Brother-in-law Sasibhooshan, Cousins Bindu, Usha,
and Vatsala, Me, and my sister-in-law Susheela.

Fig. 30: Sunset over the Himalayan peaks, reflected in The Mandakini
Ganga

Fig. 31: My doli, and Amal, one of the four young men who carried me up to the temple.

Fig. 32: Kedarnath Temple, framed by snow covered Swargarohana Mountains in the background.

Fig. 32a: Kedarnath Temple the large temple bell in front.

Fig. 33: Usha at Kedarnath, 12,500 ft. Snow covered Swargarohana Mountains in the background.

Fig. 35: Shakuntala trekking down from the temple at Kedarnath. The rails are painted with the tricolors of the Indian Flag.

Fig. 34: Shakuntala and Family at Kedarnath.

Fig. 36: Himalayan Mountain ranges, as seen on my way down from Kedarnath.

Fig. 37: Erosions in the landscape due to mudslides. The power of the rushing water cuts up the face of the mountain. Alaknanda River seen many feet below.

Fig. 38: Buses ahead of mine close to the edge of the road.

Fig. 39: Snow-laden Mountain peak above Alaknanda River.

Fig. 40: Rudraprayag, the confluence of the Mandakini and Alaknanda Rivers.

Fig. 41: Devprayag, the confluence of Bhagirathi and Manadkini Rivers, forming the Mandakini Ganga.

Fig. 43: Badrinath Temple, bank of windows framed by strings of lights.

Fig. 42: Lord Vishnu Temple at Badrinath.

Fig. 44: Shraadha ceremony on the banks of the Alaknanda River. The river can be seen at the right upper corner.

Fig. 45: Steps leading to the Alaknanda River.

Fig. 46: Fascinating perspective of a Sunrise in the Himalayas. Westward view. A half-hour before the sun rose above the east side of the mountains, the west side shone bright in the morning sun.

Fig. 48: Alaknanda River flowing down to meet Mandakini River to form The Mighty Maa Ganga.

Fig. 47: Eastward view, The Sunrise appears almost an hour later.

Fig. 49: Maa Ganga flows wide and long, in full force at Haridwar.

Fig. 50: A tall statue of Lord Shiva greeted us as we entered the Haridwar Township.

Fig. 51: Maa Ganga at Haridwar.

Fig. 52: Har Ka Pauri Bridge over Ganga at Haridwar.

Fig. 53: Preparing for the Ganga Aarti.

Fig. 54: Celebrating my rescue from Ganga Waters.

CHAPTER 5

The Ritual of Closure: Shraddha at Badrinath

October 1, 2011
Guptkashi to Badrinath

It was Saturday morning, and I woke up knowing it was my seventy-first birthday. One more year of my life on this earth. Eleven months here without my beloved Raj.

I was one who had loved to celebrate each birthday. For my seventieth birthday I had asked Raj and our daughters to please not have a surprise party for me. I handed them a list of friends and family I wished to celebrate the birthday with me. It was a great party. All our friends got to visit with Raj on that occasion. We had a family photo taken with forty two members of our clan. I remember his smile as he held court on my last birthday I shared with him, enjoying his food, especially mango ice-cream.

This was the first time in many, many years that Raj was not with me on my birthday. I knew it would not be a "happy birthday." Nevertheless it was a day to thank the almighty for one more year on this earth.

We were descending the Himalayan ranges from Kedarnath towards Badrinath Temple, dedicated to Lord Vishnu, and the third temple of the Char Dham. Vishnu is one of the three supreme deities of Hinduism. He is also known as Narayana. Along with Brahma the Creator, and Shiva the Destroyer, Vishnu is conceived as the Sustainer, or the Protector within the Triumvirate or Trimurti, of the Hindu Trinity of divinity. The three deities are the considered as different forms or manifestation of one Supreme Being.

Vishnu is the Supreme God who took manifest forms or Avatars, incarnations, across various ages or periods and appeared on earth to save humanity from the evil beings Asuras, demons. Lord Krishna and Lord Rama are the Vishnu avatars most known on earth.

I was hoping that worshipping to Lord Vishnu at his temple at Badrinath would help me shed light on my dharma on earth, meaning living one's life according to the codes of righteous conduct as described by the Hindu scriptures and sustain my strength as I continue living here without my Raj.

As we travelled toward Badrinath on our bus, my cell phone kept ringing. Birthday wishes from my daughters, sons-in-law and grandsons in the States came in all morning long as well as calls from my sister and my nieces in Trivandrum and my sister in Bombay. I tried to keep the calls short. Each call ended with "I love you," and Oommahs, kisses to you. Tender words for my ears. The distance of the continents and the miles slipped away, and their voices imparted the closeness of family. It was cozy. I replied to each of them, "Oommahs to you too."

When I stepped off the bus for lunch, Rosemary grabbed my hand. "What is with all the oommahs all morning? Can I give you an oommah too?"

"It is my birthday. Of course you can give me an oommah too." I laughed.

Now the secret was out. The previous day my cousins had discussed celebrating my birthday, and I had talked them out of it. Raj's absence was still acute, and I did not feel up to celebrating, knowing he will not be having them anymore.

Rosemary hugged me and planted an oommah on my cheek. Of course all the ladies around me had to share good wishes with me also. I was able to talk them out of any celebration, and they just said special prayers on my behalf. When evening came, all the other pilgrims had expressed birthday wishes to me as well.

On this leg of my trip, from Kedarnath to Badrinath, I got to see and enjoy the confluence of three different tributaries of River Ganges. The site of confluence is called a Prayag, and there are five main Prayags along the length of *Maa Ganga* associated with a main temple at each site the flow of the waters and the way the strength of the river builds up are impressive sights that one can never forget. To me it also symbolized my gaining strength in the flow of my own energy, which I thought I had lost when I lost Raj.

Rudraprayag

My first encounter with a Prayag was at Rudraprayag. The bus stopped for us, and we alighted on the side of the road to get a first-hand view of the confluence of two powerful bodies of flowing water, the Alaknanda and Mandakini Rivers. It was an unusual sight. The waters of the Alaknanda carry sandy silt from the mountains so appear sandy brown and opaque. The merging waters of the Mandakini have an aqua blue color that is clear and sparkling. The Mandakini comes down from rocky slopes so there is no distinctive silt and thus the water is pristine. For a long distance after they join maybe just over a mile or so, the waters run parallel retaining their colors. Then the joined, mixed waters flow on as the Alaknanda until they merge with the mighty Ganges.

The silt always brings different nutrients that help with growing vegetation, whereas the clear water is what replenishes drinking water. This principle applied to me personally in my search for cleansing, purging and sustenance I needed so badly at this point in my life.

These sights were in contrast to what I was used to when I grew up in Kerala, where the mountain ranges were totally different. Being south of the line of the Tropic of Cancer, lush tropical vegetation covered the mountains, and the blue waters of the Arabian Sea were only four to eight miles away from the mountains. Instead of the Himalayan Cedars and the other conifers I was looking at now, there were huge spreading umbrella–topped Mahogany trees and huge groves of Mango trees. Also, lower down, vast expanses of coconut palms rendered soothing green panoramas wherever we looked. Flowering trees, The Flame of the Forest, the Jacarandas, and some tall straight poplars, all graced the mountainsides. The rivers changed color depending on the range of rainfall. Some days the Karamana River close to our house flowed clear and blue. When the clouds rolled in from the ocean, the river took on a dull, slate blue color. When the torrential rains of the monsoons came, the balance in the river was very disturbed, the waters turning muddy and brown, but a day after the rains; it was back to its blue serene appearance. What a difference the mighty land called India offered, from one end of the country to another!

Badrinath

Finally we arrived at the town of Badrinath. Situated at a height of 10,200 feet above sea level, it is a wonderful spot on earth. The Alaknanda River flowing turbulently down the mountain acts as the foreground in a perfect mountain landscape with the peaks of the Nar and Narayan mountains as well as the snow-peaked Neelkanth glistening in the background. The entire place was pristine.

I put my luggage in the room I shared with Usha and proceeded toward the temple along with other pilgrims in our party. On our way we passed a variety shops carrying pooja supplies to take to temple services as well as fancy items of statuettes of deities, all sizes of brass oil lamps, incense holders, and paintings of the idols on framed mirrors, to take home with us.

Resisting temptation to load up on such stuff, we walked on and crossed a long bridge over the Alaknanda River.

The Badrinath temple loomed up ahead, well lit by strands and strands of colorful electric lights. The temple appeared different from any other I had seen. Square blocks of rooms, windows frames with red lights, the periphery touting green and blue lights, and at the very top, a bright white dome-light completed the details. The entire, sprawled-out structure glowed under white spotlights. Usually, the bright but undulating flames of oil lamps around the other temples gave an aura of surreal glow and set me in a solemn mood, ready to blend in with the divine energy in the sanctum. Not here. It was as if the temple was ready to wake me up. It said to me…look at me …look at the glow of life I want to impart to you.

Badrinath temple dates back to the ninth century. Sage Sankaracharya, the pilgrim that unified India through Hinduism and who restored Kedernath Temple, had initially discovered the Badrinarayan idol in the Alaknanda River and installed it in a small Temple near the Tapta Kund. Seven centuries later, it was moved to the spot where the current temple stands today, by the Garhwal kings.

As I approached the temple I saw rolls of steam come up from the riverfront, just before the steps up to the temple structure. The steam rose from hot springs in the Ganga. I was not totally surprised, having seen the hot springs within the cold river at Yamunotri on the first leg of my trip up the mountains. The sight of the hot springs again made me feel welcome. As I got closer, I saw shelters erected over the hot waters to offer privacy for men and women to use separate areas to take baths in the hot water. Being chilled by the cold weather in the mountain, it was tempting to take a dip in the hot waters. But I knew I had to wait until the next morning for the experience because our schedule was dictated by the planned group activities to a large extent.

We walked up the steep slope then up the steps. We entered the temple premises via an arched gate. The gate led us to a large courtyard with the main hall in the middle known as the Sabha Mandap, meaning a gathering place. The Sabha Mandap had intricately carved pillars and walls and a wide space for pilgrims to sit and pray in peace and connect with their dear Lord Vishnu. On this day we joined the many other pilgrims who were in a long line to get a glimpse of Lord Vishnu's idol from the outer courtyard.

Completing our pradakshanam, or circumambulation of the outer sanctum at this level, we entered the inner courtyard. Here there was yet another waiting line in the inner mandap, or gathering hall, wherefrom we had a closer view of the idol. After one more round of pradakshanam, we were able to get close to the sanctum sanctorum and get a distinct vision of Lord Vishnu's idol.

Vishnu's form is seen as seated crosslegged in a padmasana, or lotus pose which is the famous meditative pose. A golden umbrella was poised above the idol, shimmering brilliant in the reflected lights from the many oil lamps lit in all corners of the sanctum sanctorum and in front of the deity. Adorned in a slew of gold chains and wearing a gold crown on his head, with colorful floral garlands added around his neck, I saw the face of Vishnu through a mist of lamp light and camphor smoke. It gave me goose bumps.

Throughout our way up and down the steps, and going around, we were, like at Kedarnath, directed by a group of army guard members. This time, however, the guards wore regular clothes instead of uniforms and wore socks instead of leather boots. The modified uniforms were in respect for the holy site of the Lord's temple. Yet, they held guns under their mufti, which is the name of the camouflage when military personnel wear street clothes while they are still on duty. The added security in this region was because we were even closer to the Tibetan border than we were at Kedernath, and the Chinese were always a threat. After the invasion and takeover of Tibet by the Chinese, there were disturbances and outbursts of violence on many occasions. At the time of our visit there were no incidents of strife, but we were aware it could change at any time.

The way the idol of Vishnu is decorated for the morning, noon, and evening pooja services are in mirrored fashion as done in Guruvayoor Temple in South India, located about two hundred miles drive away from Trivandrum, my hometown. At the Guruvayoor temple Vishnu is prayed to in his form of Lord Krishna, one of his avatars. When Sage Adi Sankara revived the Badrinath temple in late eighth century, he established a routine of pooja rituals as is followed at Guruvayoor, in Kerala. As he did at Kedernath, he also established a tradition where a heritage of poojaris, or priests, from Kerala would be the presiding priest or Ravalji, at Badrinath.

That evening, our group of pilgrims was escorted to the Ravalji's quarters. The main room was a shrine for Lord Krishna. While we waited for an audience with the Ravalji we sat chanting prayers. Starting with an invocation of Lord Ganesha, the lord who removes obstacles, we sang many songs about Lord Krishna, describing his power, kindness, romantic notions and even stories of the pranks he played on his mother Yashoda when he grew up in Ambadi.

We stopped our chanting when the Ravalji arrived. We were fascinated by the way he described the rituals of the pooja services, so similar to the pooja conducted at Guruvayoor. He also told us how in the next month the services would be conducted at a different temple at five thousand feet height, because Badrinath area would be covered by seven to eight feet of snow for six months. During that period he himself would return to his home in Kerala. We received his blessings and returned to our rooms.

I felt a special glow of satisfaction in being able to converse with and be blessed by a priest from my state of Kerala from the south end of the continent at a holy place so far away at the northern-most part of the country and at the temple of Lord Vishnu, which follows the same traditions as I knew growing up. The games that Lord Krishna plays in our life never cease to amaze me.

I know I keep commenting on the distance and the difference between my birthplace in South India and the Himalayan region in the North, and the temples in both places. It is because they are truly different worlds, physically and culturally. People growing up under the hardships of the northern regions versus the relatively less arduous physical experience growing up in the south, with balmy sea breezes and constant warm temperatures, gives a certain laid-back attitude to us from the south. Not that the sea is kind to ones who make a living from the fruits of the ocean depths. But most of us need not to worry about the dangers of the deep.

Early next morning, before sunrise, I accompanied the rest of my family to the Tapta Kund, or hot springs, for a bath in preparation of doing the funeral rites for Raj, my deceased husband. The water was so hot I could not completely immerse myself in the river. I sat on the steps and gingerly placed one foot at a time to cleanse them in quick dips. For the rest of my bath, I soaked a towel in the steaming hot water and washed my hair at a bearable temperature and repeated the motion to bathe the rest of my body. There was no way I could totally submerge in the hot water to take a real bath. It was too hot for a total immersion, and I had to be satisfied, yet again, that I was blessed by the Ganges waters even though it was not a complete bath in the flowing waters of *Maa Ganga*.

We changed into dry clothes and proceeded to the temple. Up a dozen steps, at the first level we stopped at a Ganesha temple and took part in a short pooja service. As with all endeavors we propitiated Lord Ganesha first. After obtaining the blessings of Lord Ganesha, we stopped at a temple for Lord Kubera. Kubera is the treasurer of the gods and overlord of the semi-divine Yakshas, a broad class of nature-spirits, usually benevolent, who are caretakers of the natural treasures hidden in the earth and tree roots.

In a ritual of prayers to Lord Kubera, we were guided through a special offering of coins, (I chose to offer one hundred rupees in change) at the sanctum of Lord Kubera. After the coins were blessed by the treasurer God, they were returned to each pilgrim as prasadam, blessed offering.

Once we returned from the pilgrimage, I gave one blessed coin each to my daughters, sisters, sisters-in-law, nieces and other immediate family. They were to place the coin in the altars of worship in their homes. In doing so we believe it brings wealth and prosperity to all our households. I placed one in my pooja room as well.

As a Hindu, and having grown up with strong belief in the symbolism of the various pooja rituals, it was not difficult for me to place my trust in such actions. I was extremely satisfied to bring such tangible blessings to my family members.

After our pranams to Ganesha and Lord Kubera, we proceeded to the Sanctum sanctorum to pay our salutations to Lord Vishnu.

It was a special sight that greeted our eyes. For the morning services, just as in Guruvayoor in Kerala, the deity was covered with sandalwood paste, a whole array of gold chains at the neck, and a gold crown atop his head. Garlands of Tulsi leaves, holy blue basil, and various other floral garlands were used to adorn the deity. The pooja rituals followed the pattern just as in Guruvayoor, as well. Sage Sankaracharya made this happen when he revived this temple for Lord Vishnu.

I was overwhelmed with memories of the time when Raj and I prayed together at the Vishnu temple in Guruvayoor in 1976. Raj was a believer but did not buy into all the rituals at the temples. He had come with me only because he knew how strongly I believed in praying at the Guruvayoor Sanctum. And yet it was not just the support that he was rendering me. I also think he wanted to keep an eye on me on those long trips so I would not eat at the roadside shops and get sick.

I have been to Guruvayoor temple on two occasions since then, but Raj could not be there because of health reasons.

After the morning prayers at the Badrinath temple, we returned to the banks of the Alaknanda to perform a ceremony of rites and rituals to honor departed souls in our families, the same ritual our grandson, Niko, had performed in Chicago right after Raj passed.

I sat down by the shore of the Alaknanda River, alongside the rest of my family, and some of the other pilgrims. The deck was paved with slabs of rock, and washed clean. At thirty degrees, it was freezing cold, despite a light rug provided by the priest who was helping us with this very special prayer ritual. The Bali pooja, also called Shraadha, or Pithru pooja, is done to honor the souls of our ancestors.

This was a very special moment for me. Throughout most of India, only boys and men do the Bali Pooja funeral rights for the departed. The son of the deceased or if there are no sons, a grandson performs this special pooja. This is why our grandson Niko had performed the Bali Pooja at our home, under the guidance of a local poojari, priest. Now I was going to be able to do the same because in Kerala, Matriarchal rules are followed and so the women of the family are also allowed to do the Shraadha rites. Because Sage Sankaracharya had made the Kerala rituals the rituals of his holy temples throughout India, the Ravalji had given special dispensation for Kerala women visiting the temple to be allowed to do the Shraadha. If you were a pilgrim from North India, then only the men would be allowed to perform the right, but because I am a Kerala woman, I was able to perform the pooja.

The poojari, priest, at Badrinath had already prepared the ingredients for our Bali pooja. Cooked white rice mixed with sesame seeds which is the main item used for this pooja, plus basil leaves, flowers, red kumkum powder, sandalwood paste, and water for purification were provided to each of us. Sitting Hindu style, crosslegged, on the ground, I followed his instructions.

First, I rolled the cooked rice into small balls and placed them on a plate made of leaves. Following the poojari's instructions, the ritual started with our chanting mantras to invoke the spirits of my husband as well as my ancestors and his ancestors to descend from their heavenly abode to receive my special prayers and rituals to honor them. Next flowers and incense were offered as I chanted more mantras that I repeated after the poojari. After a while we were assured the spirits had accepted our offerings. Then, the rice balls, the flowers, and the remaining pooja items were placed on a second leaf-plate placed in front of me. After chanting a few more prayers, I picked up the second plate containing the food offerings, walked down to the Alaknanda River and floated the food, the flowers, and the plates into the flowing waters of the Ganges's tributary.

It was gratifying beyond measure for me to do these Shraadha rituals at this time. I had never been able to participate in this particular form of homage to my ancestors in the past. Due to then-current life circumstances I was not present when the occasion arose. When my own parents passed away in India I was living in the States and could not get back. To a non-believer, it may not mean much. But, as a true believer, it meant a lot for me to be able to do this at this time.

I almost cannot describe how it felt that I could fully honor Raj and his memory in an appropriate manner. I do know I was pleased, very pleased. I also noted that, one by one, the list of things I needed to do was being accomplished. With each act I felt lighter in spirit with the unburdening of my expected tasks.

I started feeling a new strength for the rest of the trip and for the rest of my life on earth.

The following morning, before sunup, I visited the temple again to see the daily cleansing and decoration of the idol for the day. The Nirmalya pooja is the first pooja of the day, performed at least an hour before sunrise. The Lord is still adorned with the flowers and garlands of the previous night. It is believed that after the night pooja when the doors are closed, the devas, Gods, come and worship the deity. A darshan, or sighting of the Lord who has just been worshipped by the Devas themselves is considered highly auspicious. That is the reason many pilgrims make it a point to attend this early morning ritual.

After the previous night's flowers are removed from the idol, the deity is bathed and redecorated with fresh flower garlands. Numerous oil lamps are lit and the morning pooja conducted to the accompaniment of loud singing of bhajans, devotional hymns. Many called out to the lord with overflowing emotion and unbridled fervor calling Lord Vishnu by various names: Krishnaa….,Govinda…,Narayanaa…, mostly the names were of the different avatars of Vishnu when he had come down to earth to destroy evil and promote peace and prosperity.

Mana Village

At the conclusion of our prayers at Badrinath Temple, we ate breakfast and proceeded to Mana Village about an hour away. Situated about eleven miles northeast of Badrinath is the Mana Village, which is well known because of the Vyasa Guha. This is the cave where Sage Veda-Vyasa resided while he dictated the great epic Mahabharata to Lord Ganesha, who then transcribed it for eternity.

We knew we were very close to the Tibetan-Chinese border because of the soldiers at the temple, but our bus driver informed us that were only seven short but very rocky miles away. He told us to help us understand the large ID numbers of the Indian Army settlement carved on the rocky slope. The numbers were visible for many miles. It seemed to me India wanted to remind China we were well prepared to meet any aggression. The tragic fact was that China had not only occupied the land, but had also banned the practice of Buddhism in Tibet, where their religion used to be their identity and the pillar of their whole life for many centuries.

In this region, we also saw the River Saraswathi flowing out of the mountain. It was rushing out from a cave-like opening in the side of the mountain and not just flowing over the rocks. Three kilometers down the mountain, the river merged with the Alaknanda Ganges.

The River Saraswathi was said to disappear after a short merge with the Ganges, and Indian mythology had stated for hundreds of years that the waters resurfaced in the west for a while, away from the flow of the Ganges, which flows east to the Bay of Bengal. History states the River Saraswathi disappeared under the Thar Desert, and flowed underground to meet the Arabian Sea in the west. In the past twenty years, space cameras have discovered an underground river bed that traces the flow of the River Saraswathi to the Arabian Sea. Digital enhancement studies of IRS-1C data (1995), (Indian Remote Sensing satellites) combined with RADAR imagery from European Remote Sensing satellites ERS 1/2, identified sub-surface features and recognized the palaeochannels beneath the sands of the Thar Desert. Archeological, Geothermal and Hydrogeological explorations have supported these findings. (Ref. The GIS Development. net, Geographical information Systems.)

As a child, surrounded by mythological characters and the avatars who periodically descended on Earth to fight evil, I had never questioned the existence of a disappearing river which is known to run underground in its journey to the sea. Even so, when the new evidence surfaced twenty years ago, it felt good to be validated. When I set out on this pilgrimage I did not have the faintest idea I would be seeing the origin of River Saraswathi which had once been a powerful life source in Rajasthan and neighboring States.

Close to the origins of this river there was a temple honoring Goddess Saraswathi, the goddess of learning and knowledge. It was a small shrine. I prayed in front of the deity, a serene goddess figure holding a book of Vedas in one palm, and a Veena on her lap. A veena is a musical string instrument with two resonance boxes at both ends and is played sitting down.

My eyes closed, I silently absorbed the thin mountain air into my whole body. A serene feeling came over me, and the knowledge of what I had experienced so far on this journey washed through me. I realized I did get blessings of *Maa Ganga* at her origin at Gangotri, and that I had surrendered my concerns of my future by the feet of Lord Shiva at Kedarnath so he could get rid of them. It came to me how the rites for the souls at Badrinath released my burdens in some way, and that I was empowered by Lord Vishnu to live the rest of my life without regrets.

The experience of seeing the origins of a disappearing river also gave me the insight that our inner strengths are not always overtly visible. Yet the stream of strength is there, deep within my core, to be tapped into when I needed help not just to move forward, but to move forward with meaning.

Song of the Mountains

Looking down the rocky slope upon the confluence of the River Saraswathi to the Alaknanda River, I also came to understand something that I had not been actively looking for but had focused some attention on, the song of the mountains.

I had long thought that it would come blowing in the wind between the rocky slopes which is the way I had expected to experience it. Before we boarded the bus to the Mana village, I closed my eyes and meditated. As I did, the sounds of the flowing and merging waters enveloped me with a peace I had not felt in a long time.

For the past many years it had been a whirlwind of doctor's appointments with Raj, hospital visits and long trips from one to the other. All the noises in my life added up to the humming of the cars running, the groaning and slamming of the opening and closing of car doors, "bing" sounds of elevator doors, clicking sounds of fax machines and the constant rings of telephones bearing results of tests performed and instructions for treatments to follow. I had said that while the doctor visits were like commas in our lives, the emergency room visits were like full stops or periods that interrupted the smooth flowing of our lives in the past five years.

Seated quietly on the mountain top between the rocky and gravelly slopes beside me, the regal temple below me, and the tributaries of the rivers flowing into each other, I came to the realization that the song of the mountains did not come blowing among the pines, although in itself, the sound was beautiful and unique. No, it was something more.

The song of the mountains that I had heard so much about was truly in the flowing rivers, through the gurgling rhythm of the waters, combined with the laughter of their waves on the mighty rocks, and even the occasional roar as it made some rocks tumble down the slopes. The rivulets were the first notes in a Sonata, and the flowing waters through the rocks and slopes made the rhythms of an arpeggio, and finally reached a crescendo of the symphony that was the mighty River Ganga. This was not a song for my ears alone. The music now grabbed my heart and my whole being and made me tremble at my very core.

There is the old saying, "When the mind is ready, the master appears." My mind had been rendered fragile from the incidents of the past few years, my heart had gone through the rigors of my permanent parting from Raj, and my whole being had received insults from negligence while I tended to my wounded partner. Even though I was more diligent than most in keeping my mind and body in shape, I knew the efforts were not enough. I now realized that all of me needed to be primed by my experiencing the mountains themselves, before I could recognize and experience the song of the mountains.

I had changed. I was not looking for answers. I knew I would get them when I was ready to receive.

All I needed to do now was to surrender to the mighty mountains and the powerful *Maa Ganga*, and either allow peace to seep in or accept agitation that would churn up more energy for whatever I was destined to do.

This realization was the culmination of all I had experienced in the temples and in the rivers. Now as I journeyed through the rest of our pilgrimage and eventually back to my home, I knew the song of the mountains would be the force that connects me to the universe and the flowing water it represents would be the ongoing power within me as I go on with my life.

CHAPTER 6

The Final Blessing of the Goddess Ganga: Haridwar

October 2, 2011
Badrinath to Pipalkoti, on the way to Haridwar

After my prayers to Lord Vishnu, I gathered the prasadams, blessed pooja items of flowers, fruits and sandalwood paste from the Badrinath temple and packed them away for sharing with my family in Trivandrum and Chicago.

While I had completed my Char Dham pilgrimage without any mishaps or interruption, I had a good idea of how blessed I was. But my mind did not yet process the full significance of all that I had experienced. I felt that although the pilgrimage itself was completed, my mission was not complete. I knew that I could go on with my life without Raj, and I knew that I had the blessings of the Deities to do so. What else was there?

Leaving Badrinath was difficult. I felt gratified for having done homage to Raj's spirit with the ritual of the Shraadha, which was more than I hoped for when I undertook the pilgrimage to Ganga. I also felt relieved I was going down the mountains to warmer levels.

Yet, I felt restless as if something was still missing. I could not define the yearning, but it was definitely for something more. It swam inside me like….what? I couldn't put my finger on it.

The group sitting in front of me in the bus, led by Rosemary started chanting Shiva prayers.

"Nama Shivaya paahi maam nama shivaya paahi maam…"

"Nama Shivaya paahi maam nama shivaya paahi maam…"

(I call thy name, oh Shiva, and ask for refuge…)

I joined them for a short while. My thoughts then drifted away to another bus trip in 1976 with Raj, when my sister Jayee and family from Bombay and my sister-in-law Manju and family from Bhilai joined our family to tour Delhi. In that bus trip we sang songs from our youth, light movie music that was nostalgic and melodious. The guys would insert naughty words to the real romantic lyrics, changing the connotation, and make us laugh. It also aggravated us. Those songs were special to us—how dare they change the words and the meaning?

What I would not give to relive those days with Raj, aggravation and all.

"Veruthe yee mohangal yenn-ariyum-pozhum…
Veruthe mohikkuvan… moham…."

Words from an old song spread through my mind, meaning—

"Knowing these yearnings are futile, (I) still wish to yearn for those yearnings…."

Melodious but futile and still too frustrating.

I thought as I watched the rocks in the river, memories cling like moss to river rocks.

I suddenly realized something. Memories are all I have now. Clinging to them feels good. But if I learned anything from this long and arduous journey it's that I have to make sure I don't get stuck in them, especially the good ones, and forget to move forward. That would be counterproductive. Hopefully the lessons of the flowing river will help to keep me moving and not stagnate.

The trip down was not any easier than in the previous days. The roads are not paved and are always perilous. One false move by the bus driver and over the edge we'd all go. Busloads of people have died coming down from this pilgrimage. I was just feeling like I had some stability. I didn't want to be one of those statistics.

Narrow roads carried more traffic as the towns got more populous. Small and large Lorries and more motor bikes and people on foot made our trip slower. But this also gave me the chance to see the people. Young boys and girls in school uniforms of blue and white, very similar to my grade-school uniforms in the fifties, were walking to school or waiting at bus stops. It was a universal sight, and I could see in them the young girl in me before Raj and before leaving the comforts of my Ammoomma's home.

The novelty shops and food markets by the roadside were unique. Garlands of fresh flowers woven with brilliant reds, yellow and orange were hung on slender ropes stranded atop the front entrance to the shops. Across the road rows of silk and plastic flower garlands with even brighter pinks, red and green shades competed with the real ones. Also hung on strands of ropes were varying sizes of scarves and shawls in vibrant orange and blue silks. The wild combination of the varying textures and colors rendered the open stalls along the roadside to appear unreal like kaleidoscopic visions. All this, along with the strong aromas of burning incense, mixed with pungent smells rising up from the not-too-far off water drains and the smoky, dusty streets gave me an eerie feeling as if I was out of this world. It almost felt like an out-of-body feeling that I had a hard time explaining to myself.

When I saw more car and truck service stations, I knew we were approaching major towns. It made me marvel that in all of the travel in over ten days we encountered only one difficult truck driver who refused to reverse his truck to let our bus pass so we could resume. And even there, a military truck appeared within minutes and authoritatively cleared the road and ensured progress on the path.

Yet, re-entry to real life and "civilization" were somewhat disconcerting. I was coming down, literally and figuratively from being so much a part of the pure melody of the river. As for most pilgrims, I'm sure, the song of the mountains is far more preferable than the jabbing car horns and jarring sounds of modernity.

On the way down from Badrinath, I visited Sage Adi Sankara's Ashram, Jyotir Math, also known as

Joshimath, where he had lived and taught his philosophy when he was not circling India. Living in austerity,
in a cave near the site of the present Joshimath, he had
composed volumes of prayers and also documented his
beliefs. Sri Sankaracharya had established four Maths,
or monastic orders, at the original Char Dhaams.
The remaining three principle seats of learning set
up by the Sage are located in Purī (Orissa), Sringeri
(Karnataka) and Dwaraka (Gujarat). They continue to
be centers of Sanskrit scholarship and Vedic Hindu
philosophy to this day.

The Joshimath Ashram still holds a monastery where
residents spend all day in meditation and prayers to
promote peace on earth and to ensure Hindu practices
as the Sage himself promoted. These include chanting
of mantras and prescribed prayers at different times of
the day. Prayers at dusk offering thanks for a blessed
day and for safekeeping at night are not different from
the ones I said to Jesus when I went to the Catholic
school as a young girl. It also reminded me of what
Lord Krishna said to Arjuna the troubled Pandava
prince in The Bhagavat Gita:

"Whosoever worship me through whatsoever path,
I verily accept and bless them in that way."

Just outside the cave within which Sage Adi Sankara
had lived stands a Kalpavriksha tree. The Kalpavriksha
trees are known to live from two thousand years to
twenty-five hundred years, and are attributed with
magical powers to render one's wishes.

The local folklore states the tree at Joshimath to be over two thousand years old; however, some disciples of the Sage AdiSankara states that he planted the tree, which would make it about twelve hundred years old. Regardless, what I saw was an impressive large shade tree with beautiful dark green leaves spreading over twenty feet across the face of the cave.

Within the dimly lit cave, an occasional flickering oil lamp was the only source of light. Entering the cave, I saw a statue of Sage Adi Sankara in a meditative pose. Even the sight of his statue made of white marble was soothing to my eyes. I stood with folded palms in prayer in front of a marble statue of Adi Sankara, and I received a feeling of deep peace within me. I was happy that I was standing on a site blessed by the great sage, hundreds of years ago.

Exiting the cave, I looked up at the mountains I had just descended, and the very thought of all who had gone before me and of the many who had not made it back, filled my eyes with tears of gratitude that I had come so far.

That night we stopped at Pipalkoti. This is a bustling town, has good hotels and is a hub for visitors choosing to go for ski activities to the north or water sports towards the rivers. However, we were still on our pilgrimage, so our meals were prepared by our own cooks. Naan, a type of soft flatbread, and dhal, a lentil dish flavored with turmeric and cumin was just right after a long day on the road. A cauliflower curry with red pepper and coriander completed the meal. We slept well until the morning coffee-call at four am.

There was one more stop we were scheduled to make, a very important one, Haridwar. It is one of the seven most sacred cities in all of India and its name means "gateway to God." There is a saying in India, "Agar apne paap dhone hai to Haridwar mein Gangaji ki dubki lagao," if you want to purify yourselves take a holy dip in the water of river Ganges at Haridwar. All your sins will be purified.

My mother and father went to Rishikesh and Haridwar in the sixties. They were both part of a group from Abhedananda Ashram in Trivandrum on this pilgrimage. When they arrived at Delhi, an older member of the group fell ill. My father, instead of continuing on the trip with the group, accompanied this older friend back home to Trivandrum. My mother completed the pilgrimage with the rest of the group. As she was a woman of few words, and since we did not see each other until many years after her trip, she did not share her thoughts with me. She was not one to brag, and she did not see any need to share her experiences with me.

I was too young and too pre-occupied with raising my young family to have asked her for any details. By the time my spiritual inquisitiveness was awakened, it was too late. She was gone.

Surely that is one of the reasons I am resolute to share my experiences in this pilgrimage with my daughters and my grandchildren. Whatever happens in the future, they will have my written words to know and what I have gained and how I have grown during this time. Not only my progeny but also other seekers who see a need to get over a rough and sad period in their lives will gain from my telling my story.

I strongly believe my sharing my story will show others how to grieve and say goodbye with grace and dignity, and to know that memories need to be cherished without causing them to stunt your progress.

October 3, 2014
Haridwar: The Mighty *Maa Ganga* leaves the Majestic Mountains

Haridwar is an ancient pilgrimage site situated in the foothills of the Shivalik range in Garhwal Himalayas. It is one of the primary areas where river Ganges emerges from the mountains. This is where *Maa Ganga* starts her final journey, moving full force down her path, and spreading her blessings over the plains of Northern India to join the ocean at Bay of Bengal. It is a most beautiful place. Lush green forests, gurgling rushing waters of the river Ganges, and the beauty of the mountains in the background create the charming beauty of this holy city.

Haridwar contains two words Hari and Dwar. Hari means god and Dwar means gate. Haridwar is often referred to as gateway to god, because very often the trip to Char Dham temples starts here.

Haridwar is always place of interest for the researchers because it is one of the oldest living cities in India.

It has numerous temples with interesting legacies, and it is known as the gateway for the four Dhams of the Himalayas: Gangotri, Yamunotri, Kedarnath and Badrinath—the pilgrimage that I just completed.

Apart from religious importance Haridwar, is also a centre for learning different arts and culture and is well-known as great source of Ayurvedic medicines and herbal remedies.

It has been proved by archaeological findings that terracotta culture had an existence in Haridwar during 1700 B.C. and 1800 B.C.

It was important for me that I end my own personal pilgrimage at Haridwar. There I could pay homage to *Maa Ganga* as she flows wide and regal, carrying waters from all seven tributaries from the Himalayan ranges.

After a long day of travel, we reached Haridwar Township. As my bus got closer to the center of town, the signs of increased population density were visible, including more gas stations, large marquees announcing public and private school campuses, bus depots bustling with tradespeople carrying loads of clothing and other sundries, bullocks carts carrying various vegetables in crates and baskets, and bicycles loaded in the back with large baskets of goods. The constant clanging of the cycle bells, blasting horns from the buses, the smells of all what the animals left behind, and the dust raised by this increased traffic assaulted all our senses. Fortunately, the air-conditioning was turned on in my bus, and breathing was not a problem anymore. That struck me as funny for some reason.

While travelling in the cold mountains, we certainly did not need the air-conditioning—the air was cold and pristine.

A large statue of Lord Shiva, bearing a huge Trident was visible, heralding the holy river even before we saw its fast flowing waters. Miles and miles of the river banks touted steps into the waters, which were built in the time of Emperor Asoka, between 310 B.C. and 260 B.C. Later rulers of India constantly maintained this area, leaving the steps in good shape even to this day. At about the fifth or sixth step down, metal rods and chains had been installed for safety because of the powerful flow of the river. Despite warnings by the authorities, many a daring tourist goes too far into the river, gets swept away by the currents, and drowns.

It was the last evening of my Himalayan voyage, and I was all wound up after a long day in the bus. Having unloaded our belongings in our hotel, all the pilgrims in my party walked along the banks of the vast, fast river. For about fifteen minutes we walked along the river, enjoying the sounds of the flowing water and watching the various birds including gulls by the riverside. We crossed over the waters on a bridge two blocks long.

There I boarded a cable car and was hoisted up to Bilva Parvat the next mountain, where the Mansa Devi temple is located. In this temple Goddess Parvathi is honored in the form of Mansa Devi. Manas means mind, and prayers at this temple is believed to help attain whatever your mind wishes for at the time.

And my mind wished for equanimity and peace in the remaining years of my life.

The prayers to the Mother Goddess was more meaningful on this particular day because it was the time of the annual Navaratri festival, nine nights, (and days) in the year specially dedicated to prayers for the various avatars of our Mother Goddess. The last two days we do poojas for Saraswathi Devi, the Goddess of learning, at an altar setup in our homes in her honor. For the last twenty-four hours, an oil lamp is kept lit. All items representing learning and practicing of any arts and crafts, such as text books, musical instruments like violin or veena, a stethoscope (if there is a doctor in the house), and even items used to play sports such as tennis racquets are placed at her altar overnight to be blessed by our Goddess of learning. On the tenth morning after a pooja for Saraswathi, each of us writes "ॐ"or "Ohm," the auspicious sound symbol, and then follow that by writing all the letters of the alphabet in an act of re-dedication of our commitment to learning. Once our books are annually blessed by this pooja ritual we reclaim them from the altar to resume our learning process.

Having performed this special pooja at the Mansa Devi temple, I was elated and felt hyper-energized as we made our way back to the shores of *Maa Ganga* at Haridwar. I did not hesitate even for a moment when a younger devotee edged me on to run fast with him along the three hundred and fifty feet long bridge across the River Ganges. I made it. We reached the opposite shore ahead of the rest of my family and joined in their laughter at my craziness when they caught up with us.

My *Ammoomma* had advised me sixty five years ago that it was alright to reach for the stars but to have my feet firmly planted on the ground as I did so. On that evening my feet were flying, soaring with my wish to meet *Maa Ganga* at the confluence of all her major tributaries, in all her glory, as she started her journey down to the plains of India.

My cousins and I had no plans to bathe in the Ganga waters at this site. It was getting dark when we got to the riverfront. We prepared to do the Ganga-aarti, a ritual of floating plates woven from banana leaves, filled with flowers, grains of rice and the bright flame of an oil wick contained in a little clay lamp, as the ultimate act of honoring *Maa Ganga*. All the while, as we made this special offering, we would chant "*Sarwa-mangala Mangalye…,*" a prayer to the Goddess to provide an auspicious ending.

Along with my family members I started down the steps to float my offering on the fast flowing waters. As I stepped on to the second step, Rajendran, one of our co-pilgrims, called to me, *charukkunund ketto*, it is slippery. Even as I heard his warning, I had already slipped and fallen into the water. In my enthusiasm of the process, my feet were not as well planted, and on the second step down to the waters, my left foot gave way and I landed in the river with a splash.

The offerings and the lamp floated away. I found myself totally immersed in the holy waters of *Maa Ganga*, coat, cap, purse and all. I was face down in the water. I held my breath, and in a split second pushed up on the next step with my left hand. I reached out my right hand above the water, which was immediately grabbed by our friend Rajendran, the person who saw me go down, the same one who had started to warn me. He took a firm hold of my extended arm and pulled me out of the flowing waters.

I was very fortunate. No sooner was I out of the water when many hands came with dry towels and even their dry scarves to help me dry up as much as possible.

I could not believe I did not panic and splutter. As I went under the water, I did not take in any water. I didn't choke or cough, and I had the presence of mind to extend my arm out to the voice I had last heard. I did not have time to think any bad outcomes—even though that was a very real possibility—because it all happened in a very, very short time. I do remember the pull of the currents at my feet, but I don't even remember feeling cold or scared.

Usha hugged me close. She said she heard the splash, saw me in the water, and froze. Knowing how fast the river flows, she was aware of the danger I was in. By the time she fully realized what had happened, I was already out of the water, being helped up the stairs by Rajendran. Usha sobbed as she held me tight.

Out of the water, even with a dry shawl someone had draped over me, I started shivering. I had no clothes to change into because we had left our bags in the hotel a few miles away, and we had not planned on a bath in *Maa Ganga* here at Haridwar. The whole group was scheduled to visit an Emporium for one last shopping spree before we returned to Delhi. Here, in addition to carpets, gift items, jewelry and other curios, there was a clothes section. I purchased a new outfit and changed clothes in the privacy of their "office-room."

As we sat down for our evening supper, Rajendran's wife, Jyothi, brought over a red bangle, one she had purchased from Mansa Devi Temple, the one we had visited just before we got to the Ghats at the river. She was convinced that the Goddess Devi had helped me from the waters. She wished me to keep the bangle as a blessing. We finished our evening, and I felt wonderfully, finally, at peace.

I have a very clear theory of what happened. I had dreamed since the age of eleven about taking a bath in the Ganges. After all these years, I did get the chance to take baths in the Ganges at Gangotri and at Badrinath, but it wasn't full immersion. The water was either too cold and the currents too fast at Gangotri or too hot at Badrinath where I had to dip my towel in and out of the springs and pour the water at manageable temperatures over my body to take a bath.

Maa Ganga simply decided she was not going to have this devout daughter leave her shores without fulfilling her lifelong wishes. Hence, she facilitated a slippery fall on her steps, one that immersed me completely in Her Holy Waters. I was safe even in the fast current, with the chain and fences for me to grab onto and the people surrounding me. I am still surprised I did not break a bone or hit my head and get a concussion. I did have some bad bruises and lumpy hematomas on my right leg and right forearm where I hit them on the steps. It is interesting they only started hurting the next day.

The more I think of the incident, it does not feel like a theory any more. I am convinced *Maa Ganga* fulfilled my wishes. It is as simple as that. This reiterates my belief in the powers of the Universe, the power of the elements, and the power of prayer, all of which gets revealed to me as a mortal, when the pre-destined time and place come together. It only happened when it was meant to be. I humbly thank the Almighty God, and do *pranams,* to the powers that be, for my experience.

Each experience I had in the past fortnight had given me a new perspective. I had thought I would have to rely on the strength of our love to sustain me after Raj's passing. But each segment of this journey opened up new venues and new insights into my own inner strength, as well as the power of the blessings received from the mighty mountains and the powerful waters.

Once I was fully immersed in the holy waters of the full power of *Maa Ganga*, the purpose of my personal pilgrimage was complete. The culmination of the journey I undertook succeeded in the accomplishment of my mission in gathering strength to go forward in my life without Raj. I was strong, purified, motivated and energized. There would be no one or nothing stopping me now.

My Journey Home

October 3, 2011—My Home Calls Me Back

I boarded the bus alongside my family members and the other pilgrims for the long ride back to Delhi.

Himalayas means the home of the snow. As we started our journey home, I closed my eyes and meditated. I had experienced the glory of those breathtaking mountains, the majesty of the peaks, the serene cold air. I had witnessed something I never imagined possible, the power of the waters, starting from a stream on a mountainside then building, building, ever downward gathering water, collecting strength, until all the different rivers that form *Maa Ganga* flowed together as one. It rendered me in an emotional haze.

Yes, I was lucky I was able to make the trip. But luck had nothing to do with it, really.

It was the blessing Raj always gave me: "Go if you want to. Just leave me out of it." I know it was not easy for him to give that release when he was alive. He preferred to have me by his side than off travelling the globe. Knowing that, I went any place without him only if I absolutely had to go, like when my *Ammoomma* suffered a stroke, and I had to go see her. Once Raj had his liver transplant in 1995, I did not travel without him anywhere in the world.

But as always it was his permission that initiated my plan. It was divine intervention that helped me plan it. It was my own determination that got me through to the end with all my goals accomplished. I agree it was my adventuresome nature that energized me, and the forces of the Universe helped me to mobilize members of my family to go with me. Even with his blessing the trip without him was not easy. I never stopped wishing he was with me to enjoy and accept the spirit of the mountains. But I know he is now beyond all such restrictions, above the mountains and beyond mortal boundaries.

I will be honest. I still ache every moment with his absence. The sadness still comes rolling in like waves of fog. But as I heard the song of the mountains, I knew with all my being that to succumb to it would mean to fear life itself. Our love had made me too strong for that, the same love I know now with certainty will keep me whole forever.

Since 1958 at Trivandrum Medical College, he and I dreamt, planned and lived our entire life as one team, one dream.

When he passed on, in November 2010, through my tears, I made up my mind it was in sharing him and his stories with our children and our family that

I would keep him alive. It would do no one any good to stay in silent mourning.

My Char Dham Yatra, journey to the four Dhams, in the Himalayas gave me a new perspective on our relationship.

I know now our love is truly divine and immortal. I know now that I don't need to be sad.

I can honestly now feel a difference in my outlook now—a feeling of eternity in my existence! I know it is not about my physical existence. Just as the lofty peaks of the mountains stand eternal, I too am an eternal being, and so too my dear Raj, whether our physical bodies are on this planet or not. My spiritual voyage in the Himalayan Mountains has brought clarity and purpose on my journey forward without Raj.

My surviving the fall and total bodily immersion into the holy Ganges waters without any major injury reinforced my belief in the power of prayer. Not that I had ever doubted it. It also feels like a rebirth and reaffirmation of my life on this earth. The pilgrimage was like a massive intake of a cleansing breath, with each element of the trip representing elements of closure, layer by layer.

But finally, as I rode in peace on that bus, I could exhale, cleansed, pure, and re-invigorated with life. As I opened my eyes, I felt a longing I had not felt on the entire journey, a sudden urge to return home. That massive exhale I felt was one of final closure. I knew I was ready to be back in the United States, nestled once again in comfort among my children and grandchildren.

Raj's Final Blessing

Three weeks after my return home I finally told my daughters about my fall in the waters of *Maa Ganga*. By then all the bruises had healed and they saw me safe and sound on their own turf. By then they had no reason to worry about me. Their reactions were as I predicted. Relief I returned home without any broken bones, and enough worry to ask me not to go on any dangerous trips in the future.

Many months after returning home from this incredible Pilgrimage, blessings still flow my way. The way my family and friends have nurtured me and my spirit, although not unexpected, has uplifted my outlook and made my days without my beloved Raj, bearable. The strength I have in my family is that I can grieve freely and deeply, since they have also shared the man he was, even though each family member knew him in their own and very different ways.

Reflecting on my spiritual experience on this voyage, I feel validated in what I wished to do; my Pilgrimage to *Maa Ganga* was and still is a success.

The co-pilgrims I travelled with, the temples I prayed at, the places and people I came across, and the Song of the Mountains that I heard have made me humble. Yet, there is a newfound power and perspective within me to go forward, living a conscious life filled with generous love.

I know Raj is smiling from above, and still saying, "Just leave me out of it."